VISIONS OF SPACE

VISIONS OF SPACE

ARTISTS JOURNEY THROUGH THE COSMOS

Written, compiled and designed by
David A. Hardy
with artwork by Earth's finest Space Artists
Foreword by Arthur C. Clarke

LIMPSFIELD · LONDON · NEW YORK

A Dragon's World Imprint
Limpsfield
Surrey RH8 0DY
Great Britain

First published by Dragon's World 1989

© Dragon's World 1989
© David A. Hardy 1989
© The copyright in the original illustrations and paintings contained in this book is retained by the individual artist concerned, who are listed in the Index of Artists.

No part of this book may be reproduced, or transmitted in any form or by any means, electronic or mechanical, including photocopy, recording or any information storage and retrieval system, without permission in writing from Dragon's World Ltd, except by a reviewer who may quote brief passages in a review.

British Library Cataloguing in Publication Data
Hardy, David A. (David Andrews) *1936–*
    Visions of space.
    1. Graphic arts. Special subjects. Outer space.
    I. Title
    760′.0449523

ISBN Hardback 1 85028 098 3
ISBN Limpback 1 85028 136 X

Typeset by Bookworm Typesetting, Manchester

Printed and bound in Spain by
Gráficas Velasco, S. A. - Madrid

(Pages 2–3) '*The Way It Should Have Been: A Tribute to Chesley Bonestell*' (acrylics, 18½ × 30 in/470 × 760 mm) was painted specially for this book by **David A. Hardy** to bring together the historical and modern concepts it embodies. It also makes the point that the public quickly lost interest in the Apollo missions; was this because of the drab flatness of reality compared with the dramatic visions of the early artists?
(Page 6) '*The Solar System*' by **Helmut K. Wimmer** (poster paint, 47 × 47 in/1222 × 1222 mm, courtesy of the artist) was painted as a backdrop for an exhibition of astronomical instruments.

Contents

Foreword

Arthur C. Clarke *(Courtesy Rocket Publishing Company Ltd.)*

In 1972 I wrote the following words as a foreword to a book by Patrick Moore and space artist David A. Hardy, entitled *Challenge of the Stars*:

Everyone knows the role that science-fiction writers have played in presenting the idea of space travel to the world decades — indeed, centuries — before it was actually achieved. It might well be argued that if there had been no writers, there would be no astronauts today. Before the reality, there must be the dream to provide inspiration.

The role of the space artists, however, has been much less appreciated, perhaps because there are so few of them; the good ones can be counted on the fingers. Popular books on astronomy, over the last few centuries, must occasionally have regaled their readers with space-views of the Earth and Moon. However, it was the rise of the science-fiction magazines in the 1930s that first gave the space artist a popular audience.

It must be admitted that most of the pulp-magazine artists — who had little knowledge of science, and were probably even more miserably paid than the writers — were concerned with entertainment rather than with accuracy. That both could be combined was demonstrated when *Life* magazine, in the early 1940s, published Chesley Bonestell's stunning views of Saturn from Titan, Mimas and its other moons. I can still recall the impact of those paintings — and my annoyance because some Earthbound *Life* editor had remarked of the tiny figures in Chesley's moonscapes that they were merely put in 'to give scale'. To give scale, indeed! Didn't he have the imagination to realize that some day men would actually *be* out there, looking up at the ringed glory of the most spectacular of all the planets?

Though it will be some little while yet before human explorers reach Saturn, we are now in an interesting transition period when we can compare the realities of space with the earlier imaginings of the artists. The Gemini photos of Earth, the Orbiter and Apollo photos of the Moon — these have largely confirmed, but have not superseded, the creations of the astro-painters. The camera (despite many nineteenth-century fears) failed to displace the easel on *this* planet; nor will it do so in space. In fact, we have already had one orbiting painter (cosmonaut Alexei Leonov), and there will be many others in the years to come.

But the astronomical artist, like the writer, will always be far ahead of the explorer. He can depict scenes which no human eye will ever witness because of their danger, or their remoteness in time and space. Only through the eye of the imagination can we watch the formation of the planets, the explosion of a supernova, the ball-bearing smooth surface of a neutron star, or the view of our own galaxy, looking back from its off-shore islands, the Clouds of Magellan.

Of course, the space artist can sometimes be proven wrong — but that is part of the fun. Pre-Apollo moonscapes were invariably too jagged, and few if any artists (or scientists) anticipated the softly-yielding soil of the *maria*. Nor did anyone expect Mars to be covered with craters that would have looked perfectly at home on the Moon; or a Venus that rotated backwards and was almost red-hot; or a Mercury that had sunrise and sunset. There will be other surprises to come.

I welcome this book because it provides a heady mixture of education, entertainment — and inspiration. We need the latter, now that the excitement of the Apollo programme has ebbed and so many voices are asking "Why go to the planets?" David Hardy's poetically luminous paintings are a reminder that the Moon is not the goal, but merely the beginning of *real* space exploration.

Most of the above is as true today as it was in 1972, even though we have since received masses of data and wonderful images from the Viking, Venera and Voyager probes. But when those words were written, it was also true that 'the good space artists could be counted on the fingers'. During the last ten years or so, many more young artists have come into the field (not a few of them inspired by *Challenge of the Stars*). Almost all share the same optimistic vision of a future in which Man can roam peacefully among the planets, not only of our Solar System but of other stars and galaxies.

This book brings together the best of astronomical art, both historical and current. I hope it reaches a wide audience; and to all those artists, of whatever nationality, who follow in Bonestell's footsteps (whether on the Moon or a planet or Mira Ceti) I say, 'More power to your paintbrush'.

> Arthur C. Clarke
> Colombo, Sri Lanka
> December 1988

The Old Masters

The Artists Who Led the Way

Space art, or astronomical art to use its original title, has been with us for well over a century. Yet I am surprised to find, in conversation, that many people do not know what space art is. Either it is assumed to be science-fiction art, or the more realistic examples are taken to be 'photographs' which magically appear on the printed page — even when we have not yet visited the world in question.

Some artists have always felt the need to depict scenes beyond the familiarity of their own locality, and have been inspired by the dramatic, the fantastic, the 'other-worldly' — even on our own planet. They have endeavoured to show the public what lay beyond the frontiers of their day. In the 1870s and 1880s artists like Frederick Church, Paulus Leeser and Thomas Moran travelled to the poles, to the Grand Canyon or to Yosemite or Yellowstone, to paint icebergs, aurorae, volcanoes, chasms and mountains. Space artists carry on this tradition, but they have a handicap: much as they may like to, they cannot visit the places they paint. So they visit them vicariously, in imagination.

The difference between their work and that of science-fiction artists is that while SF and (especially) fantasy art is created by the mind of the artist (or the author whose work is being illustrated), the space artist must base his or her work solidly upon fact. A sound knowledge of astronomy and astrophysics, of geology, technology and mathematics, is a prerequisite for the 'realistic' school of space artists, and even the more abstract or surrealistic painters still need to have this background, or they cross the borderline into fantasy. The latter, very valuable category has its own section, near the end.

But the bulk of this book relates to realistic or 'hard' space art, by which I mean the type that represents planetary landscapes, space hardware (vehicles, space stations and so forth), or the people who will one day walk on those alien terrains and operate those ships. The important factor in this type of art is that the scenes created must be just as believable as any terrestrial subject. This does not mean that they have to be purely photographic; style and technique are as important as in any other branch of art.

Above: A line drawing by **Lucien Rudaux** *of an observer — possibly himself. (From* How to Study the Stars *by L. Rudaux, 1909)*
Below, left: A rare three-colour engraving by **James Nasmyth** *of an eclipse of the Sun by the Earth, seen from the Moon. Note the 'halo' of Earth's atmosphere. Reddish light refracted by this reaches the Moon.*
Below: Most of **Nasmyth's** *illustrations were photographs of plaster models, like this one of Mt Pico, which rises 8000 ft/2500 m from the Mare Imbrium. Rudaux knew that it was, in fact, much more rounded in contour, but it casts a long, conical shadow. (Both from* The Moon, *1874)*

Above: 'The Earth As Seen From the Moon: Part of the Lunar Alps', as painted by the **Abbé Th. Moreux.**
Above, right: 'A Gap in the Mountain Rampart of Copernicus' by the **Abbé Th. Moreux.** (Both from A Day in the Moon, 1913)

Art and astronomy have, of course, always gone hand in hand — at least since the first use of the astronomical telescope in 1610. Before the invention of the camera all telescopic observers drew what they saw, and because of our turbulent and dirty atmosphere this is still the best way to record the detail on planetary bodies. The best observers, like the Greek E.M. Antoniadi, were skilled artists in their own right. But until the end of the last century any attempt to depict a scene on another world was little more than fantasy, or at least allegorical in nature. The illustrations by Émile Bayard and A. de Neuvill for the original edition of Jules Verne's *From the Earth to the Moon* (1865) were obviously science fiction, but were at the same time attempts to render the subject accurately according to the science of the day (which is all any of us can do).

The first space landscapes to appear in a non-fictional work were by James Nasmyth, who created both paintings and plaster models, which were photographed against a black, starry background to illustrate his book with James Carpenter, *The Moon*, in 1874. By the turn of the century, periodicals such as *Cassell's Family Magazine, Pearson's Magazine* and *Pall Mall* were publishing illustrations by artists such as Stanley L. Wood, Fred T. Jane, Paul Hardy and Dudley Hardy (not related to me, as far as I know). While science fictional, many of their illustrations are remarkably realistic.

A Frenchman, the Abbé Théophile Moreux, produced 'accurate' reconstructions of lunar scenes at about the same time, though his mountains often look more like church spires. He was Director of the Bourges Observatory, and wrote and illustrated his own books, such as *A Day in the Moon* (1913). Other astronomical artists of that period include the British illustrator Scriven Bolton, who followed Nasmyth's technique of photographing plaster landscapes, but added more detailed space backgrounds, such as the Earth in the lunar sky, and the American, Howard Russell Butler, who was an excellent painter and whose work is now in the collections of the Smithsonian Institution and the American Museum of Natural History.

Both Bolton and Moreux contributed to the magnificent two-volume *Splendour of the Heavens* (1923), along with other, lesser-known artists such as H. Seppings Wright. Bolton also worked on the *Illustrated London News* in the 1920s, where he was joined by another Frenchman, Lucien Rudaux, and later by the American Chesley Bonestell, both of whom feature often in this book. Both influenced later generations of space artists.

Artists who were working in the 1930s and who produced many excellent examples of the genre include Rockwell Kent, who worked on *Life* magazine and in 1937 depicted four alternative 'end of the world' themes, Charles Bittinger, who illustrated a *National Geographic* project in 1939, and several basically science-fiction artists, notably Frank R. Paul and Charles Schneeman. SF artists have, in fact, often doubled as space artists, with varying degrees of success. (Bonestell's work often appeared on SF magazines, but he always strongly denied being a science-fiction artist). Like Butler, Bittinger travelled with a solar eclipse expedition in order to record one of the few astronomical phenomena visible from Earth with the naked eye and produced spectacular results. More recently, US artist James Hervat emulated them.

The first space artists had only telescopic observations on which to base their reconstructions. Later they were aided by the findings of astronomers using more sophisticated instruments, such as the spectroscope, which enabled them to know what elements are present in the light from celestial bodies. Thus, Mercury was painted as having one side in eternal day and one always in a Stygian darkness, relieved only by the distant 'lamps' of Venus and the Earth. Venus could have oceans of soda water (dissolved carbon dioxide), or Carboniferous forests — even prehistoric monsters. Mars had flat, red deserts with no mountains, but with 'canals' — either watercourses or strips of vegetation which spread in the Martian spring.

Jupiter had only eleven moons, and could even be given an ice-and-fire surface, while Saturn was the only planet to possess a system of rings — a mere three or four — and one of its nine satellites was the only moon to possess an atmosphere, largely of methane. Uranus and Neptune were mere blue-green discs, and until 1930 Pluto did not even 'exist'. When it did, it had no moon.

This book shows how far astronomical art has come since those days. In a very real sense, space art has come of age. No longer stylized 'artists' impressions', the creations of today's artists are used to show how space will be developed; they present the surfaces of other worlds from angles impossible to achieve from space probes (and with greater clarity), and they depict objects which are at present 'real' only to theoretical astronomers, such as black holes and galactic cores. But their work also adorns the walls of connoisseurs and hangs in museums and art galleries. Space art is finding its own niche in the art world, just as aviation, marine or western (cowboy) art have. (There is perhaps more of a parallel with the latter, since although the actual landscapes often still exist, western artists have to use their imagination to reconstruct the past, rather than the future.)

Above, left: A rare colour painting by **Scriven Bolton** *of the Sun seen from Mercury. Like Nasmyth, he usually photographed models.*
Above: A lunar scene painted in the 1920s by **Howard Russell Butler.** *(American Museum of Natural History)*
Below: 'Jupiter As Seen From One of Its Moons', an illustration from Splendour of the Heavens *(1923). Although uncredited, from its style it is almost certainly by* **H. Seppings Wright.**
Right: 'The Curious Aspect of a Phase of Saturn Seen From One of Its Satellites'. Only Mercury and Venus can show a phase, as does the Moon, from Earth. **Lucien Rudaux** *shows that this would not be the from the moons of the outer planets. (From* Sur les autres mondes, *1937)*

Lucien Rudaux The year in which Nasmyth and Carpenter's *The Moon* was published also happens to be the year in which Lucien Rudaux (1874–1947) was born. He began as an illustrator, but his hobby of astronomy led to his joining the Société Astronomique de France at the age of 18. His observations of the planets appeared in its journal between 1892 and 1914. He founded an observatory at Donville, in Normandy, and produced a photographic map of our Milky Way galaxy. From 1900 magazines such as *Je Sais Tout* and *Illustration* published articles by him, illustrated with his own accurate impressions of landscapes of other planets. As an observer, he often concentrated on the edge or 'limb' of the Moon, so he knew that the lunar mountain ranges are rounded and eroded from micrometeorite impacts and extremes of temperature. This is the way he painted them in his landscapes, creating a sometimes startling resemblance to subsequent Apollo photographs.

Although his work has the appearance of water-colour or gouache, astronomer/artist William K. Hartmann has suggested that Rudaux might have used thin oils. He worked to a very small scale, and often in monochrome because his paintings would be printed this way as book illustrations. His style is quite impressionistic, but his detailed knowledge of the subject matter combined with his skill as an artist to produce truly realistic scenes. He took great care to calculate the relative size of a planet or the Sun in the sky, the shadow cast by the rings of Saturn upon the planet itself, and so forth. As well as working for the *Illustrated London News*, he wrote illustrated articles for the *American Weekly* supplement, covering such subjects as other solar systems, alien life and the end of the world (a subject which has fascinated a number of space artists, whose work also carries them back to the beginning of time).

Rudaux also produced a number of books, of which at least three are considered to be classics: *Le Manuel pratique d'astronomie* (1925), *L'Encyclopédie Larousse de l'astronomie* (1948 — continued after his death by Gérard de Vaucouleurs), and, most famous of all because it is the first book of space art, *Sur les autres mondes* (1937). The Larousse encyclopedia was translated into several other languages, including English.

Lucien Rudaux was a council member of the Société Astronomique de France, and a member of both the Comité National d'Astronomie and the prestigious Union Astronomique International (generally known as the IAU). He was made a Knight of the Legion of Honour in recognition of his contribution to astronomy, and a crater on Mars has been named after him — perhaps the ultimate honour.

Above, left: **Rudaux** demonstrates how even low hills can cast long black shadows on the Moon when illuminated by a low Sun, and right how the valleys remain in shadow while the peaks are illuminated. (From Sur les autres mondes, 1937)
Below: A line drawing by **Rudaux** of his own observatory. (From How to Study the Stars, 1909)

Chesley Bonestell Whether or not they have heard of Rudaux, people with the least interest in space art know the name of Chesley Bonestell, since he is without doubt the most influential artist to date. Bonestell (the name could even be translated as 'good star'!) was born on New Year's Day, 1888, in San Francisco, of a Spanish-Catholic family on his mother's side and an American-Unitarian family on his father's. (In later life Bonestell became an agnostic.) As the artist Ron Miller has pointed out, the Wright Brothers were then only 17 and 21, H.G. Wells was 22 and as yet unpublished, and Jules Verne was only halfway into his writing career. . . . SF was still in its infancy.

Bonestell's first painting of Saturn, done when he was 12, was destroyed in the San Francisco earthquake and fire of 1906. Rejecting his grandfather's wishes for him to become a businessman, he studied art in the evenings at Hopkins Art Institute, and in 1911, after studying at Columbia University, New York, became an architect. This stood him in good stead when, in 1922, he went to England and worked on the *Illustrated London News* and did advertising work for Lyons Restaurants. In 1938 he began work at RKO as a

A dramatic painting by **Chesley Bonestell** *of a landing by a winged, nuclear-powered spaceship. Earth (70 times brighter than the Moon in the same phase) illuminates the scene, while the Sun rises on the mountains. (From* The Conquest of Space, *1949, courtesy of Space Art International)*

'Exploring the Sinus Roris' by **Chesley Bonestell.** *A convoy of tractors descends a crater wall. Again, Earth light illuminates the scene, except for the distant crater-wall. (From Conquest of the Moon/Man on the Moon, 1952, courtesy of Space Art International)*

special effects or 'matte' artist, and worked on films such as *Citizen Kane* and *The Hunchback of Notre Dame*. But it was his work with producer George Pal on *Destination Moon*, *When Worlds Collide*, *War of the Worlds* and *Conquest of Space* that used his talents as a space artist.

His first published astronomical art was a series of paintings of Saturn from its moons in a 1944 edition of *Life* magazine. He worked in oils, usually

in two coats, on hot-pressed Whatman board, often quite small, and occasionally over photographs. But he also produced several murals, including the 8 × 33-ft/3 × 12-m one at the Boston Museum of Science. Among several books containing his work is the famous *Conquest of Space* (1949). Chesley Bonestell died on 11 June 1986. In 1985 an asteroid was named after him.

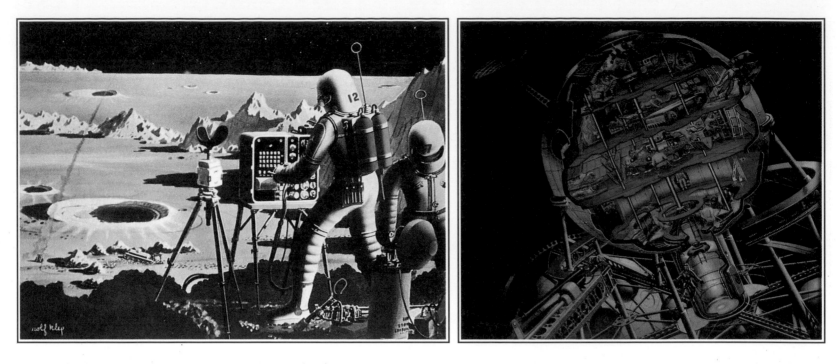

The *Collier's Space Programme* In 1950, as a result of an Army symposium on space problems held in San Antonio, Texas, the associate editor of *Collier's* magazine, Cornelius Ryan, assembled a team consisting of Dr Wernher von Braun (engineer), Dr Fred Whipple (astronomer), Dr Joseph Kaplan (physicist), Dr Heinz Haber (expert on space medicine), Oscar Schachter (expert on space law), Willy Ley (science writer), and artists Chesley Bonestell, Fred Freeman and Rolf Klep. The aim was to show a US public, whose lives were dominated by Korea and the Cold War, how human beings could move out into space.

They succeeded spectacularly. From a 'baby satellite' to a full-scale, 250-foot wheel-shaped space station and a fleet of three moonships built in orbit, the team convinced the USA, then the rest of the world, that space travel could become a reality, and created a climate in which the National Aeronautics and Space Administration (NASA) could begin its work.

Above, left: **Rolf Klep** *showed how 'moonquakes' would be caused by explorers in order to find out the structure of the Moon, for the Collier's articles. Klep is now deceased, and his art is held by the National Air and Space Museum.*
Above: **Fred Freeman** *(1906–87) prepared most of the diagrammatic work for the Collier's articles; here he shows the crew-sphere of a moonship. (Collection of Randy Lieberman)*
Below: *'Sunrise in Space' by* **Fred Freeman**. *An astronaut lies on his acceleration couch, with a view of Earth through the window. (From* This Week *magazine, September 1958; collection of Frederick I. Ordway, III)*

Above: **Mel Hunter** painted this dramatic scene of the interior of a lunar crater for Time-Life. He was born in 1927 and did his first space art for Galaxy magazine in 1954. He later worked for the Northrop Aircraft Company on their Snark project. He now lives in Burlington, Vermont, and makes original lithographs of natural subjects, such as birds and landscapes. (Courtesy of the artist)

Below, left: A winged spaceship lands on the Moon, as painted by **Jack Coggins** for Rockets, Jets, Guided Missiles and Space Ships (1951), one of his two books with Fletcher Pratt. Jack was born in London but went to the USA as a child. He did many war paintings for Life, and later worked for SF magazines like Galaxy and the Magazine of Fantasy & Science Fiction. He lives in Pennsylvania. (Courtesy of the artist)

Below, right: This fine airbrush version of von Braun's 'wheel' was **Alex Schomburg's** first cover for the Magazine of Fantasy & Science Fiction, January 1953. (Courtesy of the artist)

Science and Fiction Bonestell's *Life* magazine paintings appeared, with other works, in the book *The Conquest of Space*. The *Collier's* articles were collected and edited into *Across the Space Frontier* (1952), *Conquest of the Moon* (1953 — *Man on the Moon* in the UK) and *The Exploration of Mars* (1956). Unlike Rudaux, Bonestell believed for many years that the Moon's mountains must be 'broken and sharp'. As a result, he created his own Moon with spectacular peaks and flat, cratered plains. And other artists, especially on science-fiction covers, seized upon this. While creating often completely original scenes, they depicted not the 'real' Moon but Bonestell's version of it. . . Is it possible that this led to disillusionment when the Apollo photos appeared?

Artists who combined SF and space art (because pulp magazines were the main market in the 1950s) include Mel Hunter, Alex Schomburg and Jack Coggins (page 17), all of whom produced excellent work. Schomburg, although over 80, still paints, and is a master of the airbrush (which Bonestell did not use); his work is collected in *Chroma* (1986).

Others artists in the USA with their own individual style include Ken Fagg, Frank Tinsley, an aviation and science reporter who wrote and illustrated his own books on space travel, and Edward (Ed) I. Valigursky (1926–), who produced cover art for SF magazines, including a series of Solar System landscapes and other space subjects for *IF: Worlds of Science Fiction*. He produced his first space art in 1952, and several examples of his work appear in this book. Neither should we forget the names of Dember, Pederson, McKenna, Emshwiller (Emsh), Ebel or Wenzel, all of whom made their contributions to the genre but whose full names were never given.

R.A. Smith Ralph Andrew Smith (1905–59) is best known for his work with Arthur C. Clarke and the British Interplanetary Society (BIS) in the 1950s. He illustrated Clarke's *Interplanetary Flight* (1950), *The Exploration of Space* (1951) and *Exploration of the Moon* (1954), and his work can now be found in the BIS collection *High Road to the Moon* (1979).

Smith painted only to commission, never for his own satisfaction, and rarely produced anything other than space art. Like Bonestell, he had architectural training, but he was also an engineer and produced most of the designs for the lunar and ferry craft which are today associated with the BIS, who now own his work. He was thus a true 'first-generation' space artist — his work was all his own. His painting of a space station in orbit was used in *The Perspectivist* magazine as an example of perspective drawing.

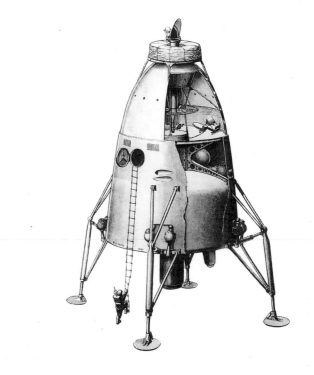

Above: One of the first of **R. A. Smith's** paintings to be seen by the public was this 'Moon Landing', painted for Clarke's The Exploration of Space (1951). Astronauts film the landing of a second ship, and a radio aerial has been erected.
Right: In this close-up scene of the first lunar base, solar generators are being erected for power. Smith was an engineer, and took great pains to ensure accuracy. (R. A. Smith illustrations courtesy British Interplanetary Society, London)

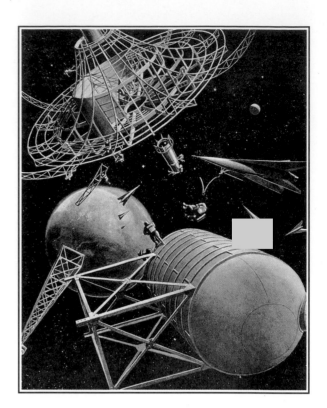

Space Craft
The Nuts and Bolts of Space Art

2

NASA's manned space programme began with canisters which went into orbit, or to the Moon, then made splash-landings, uncontrolled, in the ocean. The scenario planned by von Braun and his team, or by Clarke, Smith and the BIS, was quite different. First, to build a space station ferry craft would deliver prefabricated sections of it into Earth orbit at an altitude of up to 1025

Above, left: *'Third Stage Separation', a painting done by* **Chesley Bonestell** *for* Collier's *and later used in* Across the Space Frontier *(1951). At this point the ferry rocket is 40 miles/64 km above the Pacific; the second stage, its motors glowing, will be returned by its ribbon parachute to splash down for later recovery, as did the first. (Courtesy Space Art International)*
Above: **R. A. Smith's** *highly-acclaimed painting of the construction of a mirror-type space station, from* The Exploration of Space.
Left: *A very early painting in poster colours by* **David A. Hardy,** *who was in the RAF at the time. (It was three years before he acquired his first airbrush.) The painting was for an (abortive) early version of* Challenge of the Stars *(1954) but was never published, until now. He used elements from von Braun — the wheel — but designed his own shuttlecraft, with wider delta-wings than Smith's. The dumb-bell-shaped nuclear vehicle was designed by Clarke for interplanetary missions.*

Artist Profile

KEITH PAGE

Keith Page was born in Surrey, England, in 1951, and lives there still. He was educated at Bexley Grammar School, and became a member of the Society of Industrial Artists and Designers (MSIAD) in 1985.

He became interested in space art after seeing the work of Chesley Bonestell and other artists in *Across the Space Frontier*, but was also a fan of Frank Hampson's famous creation 'Dan Dare' in the *Eagle* comic. As a result he now also produces comic strip-type artwork, as the experimental piece on this page shows. He feels that this field has been consistently underrated, and that it could eventually be developed into a form of fine art — a goal at which he is aiming.

Working in gouache or acrylics, Keith's first published work was for children's magazines. He now also produces covers for science-fiction books, and his work appears in Germany and other European countries. He considers himself an illustrator, but produces fine art when he has time, and is developing a fine-art approach to space subjects. He also plans a realistically illustrated book on a Mars expedition. His work has appeared in exhibitions locally.

miles/1650 km. Von Braun's design was a wheel (still the most popular), while Smith's was a huge concave mirror which concentrated solar energy to produce power.

Then lunar vehicles would be launched, probably from Earth orbit; once landings were made a lunar base would be set up, growing from simple beginnings with inflatable pressure domes or discarded fuel tanks into settlements with their own ore-processing plants and hydroponic gardens to produce food as well as oxygen. That dream is not dead; it is just taking a little longer to realize than many of us hoped. And today's space artists are constantly showing, just as Bonestell, Smith and the others did in the 1950s, how we now believe it can be achieved.

The type of craft then envisaged to go into orbit was, in fact, following a parallel development. As has been dramatized in the 1983 film *The Right Stuff*, rocket-propelled aircraft such as the Bell X-1 and X-15 pushed up the altitude and speed records, and led directly to today's Space Shuttle. It was realized that to achieve a re-useable craft, wings would be needed. Von Braun

Above: A dramatic angle on the launch of the Space Shuttle by **Paul Hudson** (acrylics; courtesy Orbital Sciences Corporation).

Right: 'Morning Launch' by **Kim P. Poor** also shows the Shuttle still inside our envelope of atmosphere (acrylics, 19 × 15 in/480 × 380 mm, courtesy Novagraphics). It would be impossible to obtain either view as a photograph.

Left: 'Space Shuttle Launch' by **Keith Page** (acrylics, 33 × 26 in/850 × 650 mm). A 'fine art' rather than illustrative approach.

Artist Profile

KIM P. POOR

Kim Poor was born in 1952. He lives in Tucson, Arizona, and gained a BS in political science and classics; he has no formal art training. Kim uses his middle initial because there is another artist called Kim Poor, who is a female British artist.

His influences in space art came from the early Bonestell books and Hardy's *Challenge of the Stars*, as well as films containing Bonestell's work and television programmes by Carl Sagan. His own work was first published in the April 1981 issue of *Discover* magazine. He considers himself to be 75 per cent fine artist, 25 per cent illustrator, and 'disdains SF'. He has contributed to Sagan's *Cosmos* TV series and *Comet* book, and done work for Time-Life books.

Kim considers his major works to date to be a scene of Saturn from Dione and 'Attitude Hold', which is reproduced here. He produced a panorama for the National Air and Space Museum in Washington in 1981, and his work has hung in the IAAA exhibition, 'Other Worlds', and in the Moscow show. Among those who own examples of his work are Carl Sagan, Clyde Tombaugh and other astronomers, as well as astronauts such as Joe Allen and Harrison Schmitt.

An ex-President of the International Association for the Astronomical Arts, he runs his own company to market fine-art prints, Novagraphics (see page 39), and aims to make space art a major art-form by the year 2001.

23

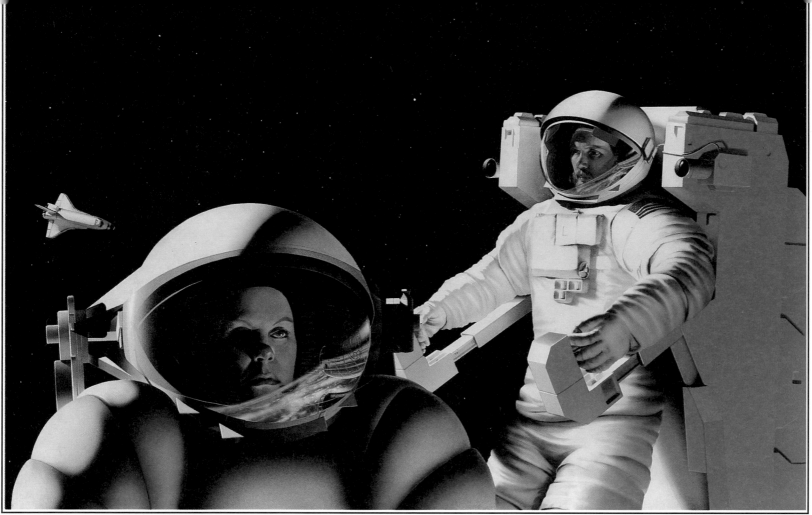

Above: 'Space Engineers' by **Pamela Lee** (acrylics; courtesy of the artist). Helmets with LCD Heads-Up Display (HUD) or Fibre Optic Photo Display (FOPD) will be needed by builders of the space station, along with Hard/Soft Suits and Manned Manoeuvring Units (MMU). Left: 'Attitude Hold' by **Kim P. Poor** (acrylics, 19 × 23 in/480 × 580 mm, courtesy Novagraphics.) In this an astronaut is wearing an MMU, enabling him to 'fly' freely in space at a fixed attitude (not altitude).

Artist Profile

PAMELA LEE

Pamela Lee lives in Modesto, California, and is a graduate of the University of Arizona.

She is the first American artist to have paintings flown aboard the Space Shuttle, and is a member of NASA's Fine Arts Program. Her painting of the 51-I Shuttle mission was selected by the Smithsonian Museum for inclusion in 'Visions of Flight' — a world tour of NASA-commissioned fine art. Her work is in the private collections of several astronauts and scientists, as well as public collections, including the Yuri Gagarin Museum in Star City, USSR, and the Pushkin Art Museum in Moscow.

A strong advocate of international cooperation with the Soviet Union, Pamela has visited space facilities throughout the USSR as a guest of the Soviet government, and is currently collaborating on a series of paintings with leading Soviet artist Andrei Sokolov. Her work appeared in the television programmes *Cosmos — Year of the Comet, Future Flight, Visions of Other Worlds* and *Beyond 2000*, among others. It has also appeared in numerous books and magazines in the USA, as well as the Soviet Union, and she co-authored, as well as co-illustrated, *Out of the Cradle* (1984) and *Cycles of Fire* (1987) — see pages 94 and 175.

Pamela Lee is currently developing an international children's collaborative art project called the Space Bridge, and executing commissions for NASA.

opted for a 'canard' design, with short, stubby wings at the front and long wings at the back of a streamlined, conical vehicle (which was itself the third stage of a 260-ft/80-m vehicle, and had five rocket motors producing 270 tonnes total thrust). R.A. Smith's ferry craft had narrow delta wings, making it resemble more closely the modern Space Shuttle.

Today we are accustomed to seeing views of the Earth from orbit, as satellite pictures often appear in weather forecasts. Several books containing photographs taken by astronauts at various heights have been published, and as a result we know what our planet looks like from space — by day and by night, at sunset and at sunrise. We know how the Moon appears when seen through our thin layer of atmosphere, how aurorae appear near the poles, how oceans, vegetation and desert look (often transmitted in various wavelengths, such as infra-red).

The early space artists had no such aids. Knowing the altitude, it was possible to calculate how much of the Earth would be seen through a determined angle. Bonestell developed a form of spherical perspective in order to show the surfaces of the Earth, Moon or Mars from various altitudes. He considered the planets as a series of flat planes 1–10 miles/1.6–16 km square, depending upon the elevation, with their centres tangent to the globe. It was then simple to find the horizon line and vanishing point of the sides of each square, and to plot the physical features of the relavent world on the squares.

He also constructed models of space vehicles out of transparent plastic, working from sketches drawn by von Braun on engineer's graph paper. His courses at Columbia University in descriptive geometry, shades and shadows and perspective, proved invaluable in helping him to solve some very complicated problems, while his courses in structural engineering helped him to understand the mechanics of space hardware. In order to meet the

'Bringing in the Big Boy' by **Pamela Lee** (acrylics, courtesy of the artist) shows Shuttle astronaut William Fisher watching the capture of Leasat 3. Reflected in his faceplate is the Shuttle, with its remote manipulator arm tethering astronaut James van Hoften to its port side, and his own life-support system controls.

Left, top: 'Challenger's Glory' by **Chris Neale** (acrylics on canvas covered board, 30 × 24 in/762 × 610 mm; courtesy of Denham Fine Art)
Left, below: 'Shuttle Re-entry' by **Douglas Chaffee** (acrylics, 16 × 22 in/406 × 560 mm, courtesy of the artist): an early stage of heating.

Artist Profile

CHRISTOPHER NEALE

Chris Neale was born in 1958 and lives in Tadworth, Surrey. He is basically self-taught as an artist.

He became interested in space as early as the age of five, being heavily influenced by the Apollo programme and the film *2001: A Space Odyssey*. He started to collect books containing the work of space artists around 1980, and particularly enjoys the work of British SF artists Peter Elson and Chris Moore, and the American, Syd Mead. He started painting himself after the success of the movie *Star Wars*.

Chris's first commission, in 1983, was to paint a lunar landscape for Thorn Ericsson Telecommunications. His major work to date is 'Challenger's Glory' (shown here), which he painted in 1986 to commemorate and capture the former glory of what was reputed to be the astronauts' favourite Shuttle. This was reproduced as 850 signed colour prints by Denham Fine Art, and signed by astronaut Robert Overmyer, one of the seven commanders who flew *Challenger*.

Chris Neale's objective is to produce images that look real, to go (boldly?) where cameras cannot go, and to take ideas and turn them into reality. He uses gouache or acrylics, and sometimes an airbrush, but dislikes over-use of this instrument.

deadlines set by the *Collier's* project, though, he would photograph the models from various angles and trace enlargements on to Whatman board in the required composition.

R.A. Smith never attempted to paint the surfaces of planets with heavy atmospheres, as he said he was not prepared to guess at their conditions and topography. He painted only the Earth, Moon and Mars, apart from one or two science-fictional subjects which were intended for magazine covers but never published. (Versions of his designs did, however, appear on the covers of the British magazine *Authentic Science Fiction* around 1953, illustrated by an artist called Davis — first name never given. This magazine also ran a series of Bonestellian planetary landscapes, painted by Davis, art editor John Richards or artist E.L. Blandford.)

Smith would study lunar maps and photographs before starting on a painting of the Moon, decide which location best suited his requirements, and adjust his elevation and viewpoint. He used his imagination only to the extent needed to portray fine detail and colour on the surface. When painting views of the Earth seen from orbit or from space he used a geographical globe, together with photographs of cloud formations taken by captured V-2s, Vikings, or sounding rockets such as Aerobee. Most of the latter tended to be soot-and-whitewash images.

This technique enabled Smith to become one of only two or three artists to predict correctly what the Earth would look like from space. He also painted a view of Earth during an eclipse of the Sun, with the Moon's

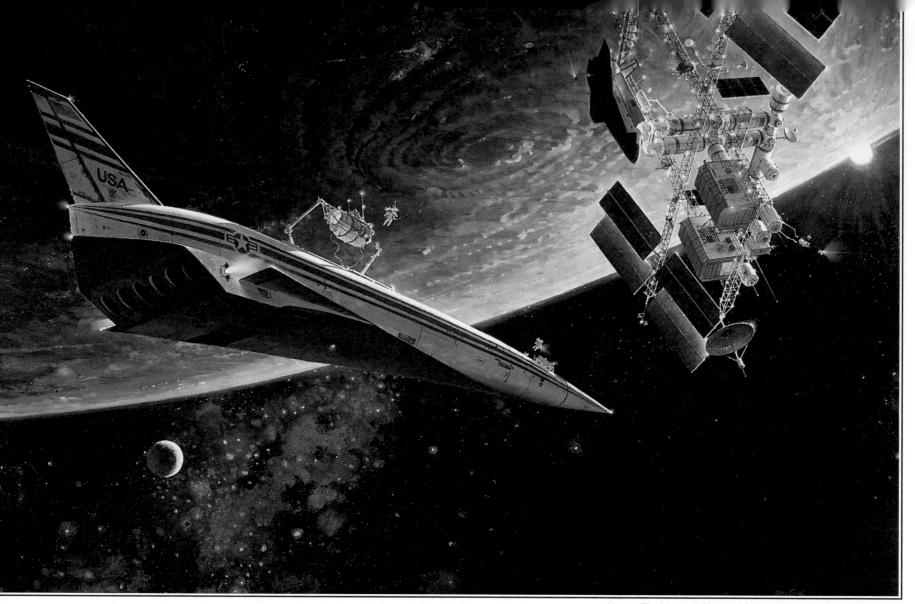

Above: 'The Aerospace Plane and Freedom Space Station' by **Robert T. McCall** (acrylics on canvas, 48 × 72 in/1220 × 1830 mm, courtesy of the Honeywell Corporation).

shadow covering Indonesia. (In the 1930s Rudaux attempted to reconstruct the Earth as seen from space, and some 20 years later, William Palmstrom did so quite accurately for the *National Geographic* magazine.) To render Mars, Smith had another globe on which he had painted the Martian features, working from photographs and observers' drawings. He drew and painted rapidly, often completing a quite complicated subject in two evenings, working in his oldest clothes and shirt-sleeves, chain-smoking and drinking tea almost continuously. When asked how long it took *him* to produce a painting, Bonestell would reply: 'Seven days to 70 years! Seven days to paint the picture and 70 years to learn how to do it.'

Although much more aesthetically pleasing than the blunt-nosed, tubular spacecraft that preceded it (and the Soviet shuttle is remarkably similar in appearance), the present Space Shuttle is not the answer to all our dreams — or our problems. The cost of launching 1 lb/0.5 kg of cargo into space is somewhere between £2000 and £4000/$3500 and $6500, largely because of the long delays between launches and the number of staff (some 5000) who need to be retained to attend each launch. This cost is actually *more* than the expendable Saturn V of the late 1960s! During the next 15 years, therefore, we can expect to see the appearance of different and more economical launch vehicles, as well as more powerful ones. The Mark II Shuttle will emerge, and also spaceplanes of the HOTOL type, like the US National Aerospace Plane (NASP or X–30), which should begin runway-to-orbit flights by 1996.

With such projects on the drawing-board, it naturally falls to the space

Artist Profile

ED BUCKLEY

Ed Buckley was born in 1940 and lives in Glasgow, Scotland. He obtained a Higher School Certificate in art and English, and works at Kelvingrove Art Galleries.

In 1948 he was given a children's book which sparked off his interest in space, and this volume was followed by Bonestell's *Conquest of Space* borrowed from a library. He first produced his own space art in 1957, and his work was first published in 1974. He worked, together with fellow-Scot Gavin Roberts, on several books by Duncan Lunan: *Man and the Stars* (1974), *New Worlds for Old* (1979) and *Man and the Planets* (1983).

Ed's work was included in the exhibitions 'Beyond this Horizon' in Sunderland in 1973, 'The High Frontier' in Glasgow, 1979, and 'Prelude to the Stars' in Glasgow, 1989. He considers himself mainly a fine artist, preferring to paint spacescapes featuring spacecraft of his own design, but will illustrate other people's ideas if they attract him.

Like many other artists in this book, Ed sees himself 'carrying the fire' and sparking an interest in space among others. He says, 'I have had so much excitement, downright enjoyment and educational stimulation from space that I want others of my own generation, or younger, to experience it too.' He is creating an illustrated 'future history' of paintings, including the technology of interplanetary, then interstellar flight, and also believable aliens.

(Page 29) 'HOTOL Being Serviced by Ground Crew' by **Keith Page** (acrylics, 21 × 15 in/530 × 380mm, courtesy of the artist). This was painted soon after the announcement of HOTOL, so differs considerably from later versions. But such horizontal take-off and landing space-going vehicles are inevitable for the future.

Right, top: 'Shuttle '61' by **Ed Buckley** (poster colour, 1961, courtesy of the artist) is an early prediction of a ferry vehicle with cargo doors. Note that it is dropping a lower stage with four large solid boosters. Right, below: Ed's 'Mixed-mode Single-stage Shuttle' (acrylics, 1975, courtesy of the artist, from Man and the Planets, 1983) was propelled by liquid oxygen (lox)/kerosene, then liquid hydrogen/oxygen. Similar 'supershuttles' are under development.
(Pages 32–3 'I Love an Astronaut' (left) and 'Tumbling Astronauts' (colour pencil, 1988, and acrylics, 1983, courtesy of the artist) show **MariLynn Flynn's** sensitive portrayal of the human aspect of space exploration.

Artist Profile

ROBERT T. McCALL

Bob McCall was born in 1919 in Columbus, Ohio, and now lives in Paradise Valley, Arizona.

As a schoolboy he lost himself in *Popular Science, Startling Stories, Amazing Stories, Thrilling Wonder Stories* ... As the next best thing to becoming an astronaut, he wanted to become a pilot. The fact that he is slightly colour blind in the red-green range meant that, when he enlisted in the Army Air Corps during World War II, he became a bombardier instead. After his service he and his new wife Louise (also an artist) went to Chicago, where he hoped to become an advertising artist as the first step to becoming a first-rank illustrator. In the mid-1950s, through the Society of Illustrators, he was one of several artists invited to visit various air bases and produce paintings which would be added to the US Air Force collection. This led to his becoming a leading aviation artist, which in turn enabled him to visit other countries, including the great museums of Europe. He produced 45 paintings in all for the Air Force.

Early in the 1960s Bob produced some paintings of future spacecraft for *Life* magazine. A few years later Stanley Kubrick invited him to England to paint posters advertising *2001: A Space Odyssey*, and consequently he met Arthur C. Clarke. Bob's image of the huge double-ring space station is probably even better known than Bonestell's earlier vision of a space-wheel, and the assignment led to a change of direction in his career — from aviation artist to space artist. His work probably appears in smaller and larger formats than any other artist's, for he has produced postage stamps and massive murals such as the one in the Smithsonian's National Air and Space Museum in Washington, DC, which took two years to complete.

Bob chronicled the development of the US space programme through Mercury, Gemini, Apollo, Skylab and the Shuttle. Isaac Asimov has called him 'the nearest thing to an artist-in-residence in outer space'. During the summer of 1988 he spent ten days working with Soviet artist Andrei Sokolov in his Moscow studio on a 10 x 5-ft/3 x 1.5-m painting to be completed in McCall's own Arizona studio later in the year. Admitting that it is not easy for two artists and two egos to work together, Bob sees the collaboration as a metaphor for the larger challenge of two superpowers attempting major joint manned space missions. And all the artists in this book will agree with that sentiment.

Artist Profile

MARILYNN FLYNN

Born in 1954, MariLynn Flynn lives in Flagstaff, Arizona, though she was born in Windsor, Ontario, and grew up in a suburb of Detroit, Michigan. She obtained a diploma from Bannf School of Fine Arts, Alberta, Canada, and also attended the Academy of Art, San Francisco, and Ontario College of Art.

MariLynn has always wanted to be an astronaut. Not being able (yet) to fulfil that ambition, she took up flying and obtained her private pilot's licence. She enjoys flying because it enables her to move in all (known) dimensions, and she is able to scout out interesting locations in the desert for later sketching expeditions. Her husband is also a professional pilot.

She has painted professionally since 1980 and considers herself a 50:50 blend of fine artist and scientific illustrator. She believes 'Tumbling Astronauts' (above) to be her major work to date, but the largest is a mural of Mars at Alamogordo Space Museum. She also paints Earthly landscapes and occasional SF art, when commissioned. Her work has appeared in many publications, including *Astronomy* and *Science Digest*, Isaac Asimov's 'Library of the Universe' series, and *National Geographic* filmstrips. It has also been shown in many exhibitions in the USA and Canada, including the American Museum/Hayden Planetarium, New York City. Her ambitions include seeing a volcano erupt ('preferably under my feet'), to make a sculpture out of molten lava — and to paint from orbit, or the surface of another planet.

artist to translate these into a form which planners can show to their financial backers, or governments to the public. It is important to keep looking towards the next century. An aerospace plane of the HOTOL type needs to be developed, if only because the present 200 tonnes per year carried into orbit is expected to double every ten years or so. It is also essential in order to construct a useful and viable space station. Dr Patrick Collins of Imperial College, London, has suggested that space tourism need not wait for space stations to be built for scientific or industrial purposes, but that it could work in reverse, with the profits from space tourism opening up space for other purposes (*Analog*, June 1988).

Just think how many people would like to be able to emulate the astronauts in MariLynn Flynn's intriguing painting above, and enjoy zero-gravity games. These are limited only by the imagination — try it! Tourism on Earth is a giant industry, and people are paying large amounts to visit more and more adventurous places. Who will be the first to construct the initial, modest modules of the first space hotel? How many people would pay, say, £6000/$10,000 for a trip into orbit? (But then, who in the 1920s could have forecast one million tourists flying abroad *every day*, and a tourist industry with a turnover exceeding £60 billion/$100 billion per year, with an annual growth rate which will double by the turn of the century?)

Chesley Bonestell

Space Stations

Stepping-stones into Space

3

As seen earlier, the first space-station designs were often simple and symmetrical. Von Braun's wheel was widely adapted (a more sophisticated version was used in the film *2001: A Space Odyssey* (1968), on which artists Robert T. McCall and Harry H.-K. Lange worked in various capacities). Ed Valigursky often illustrated a spherical type, a sphere having the greatest

*One of **Chesley Bonestell's** most famous images: the arrival of a supply ship at von Braun's wheel-shaped space station. On the left, near the third-stage rocket ship, is an astronomical observatory (forerunner of the Hubble Telescope) and two 'space taxis'. The space station is above a point 800 miles/1290 km south by east of the Galapagos Islands; the horizon is 3000 miles/4800 km away.*

internal volume and being best able to contain air pressure. R.A. Smith's favourite, which he designed with H.E. Ross of the BIS, was a giant parabolic mirror, also spinning to produce artificial gravity at the rim by centripetal force. Others favoured a spinning disc. But most agreed that space stations would 'grow by accretion', as Clarke called it — that is, bits or modules would be tacked on until the result is a sort of orbiting city.

The first space station, launched by the USA on 14 May 1973, was Skylab. Frank Kelly Freas designed the crew insignia (shoulder patch), which was a stylized version of his painting on page 37. In the event, however, one

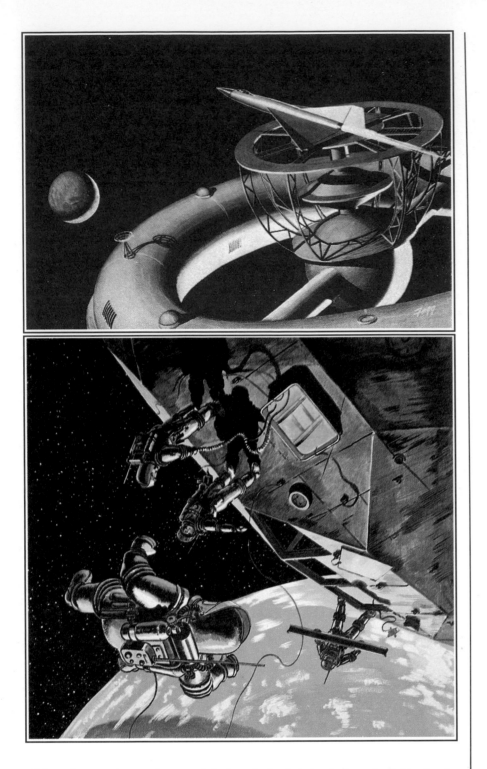

of the solar panels was damaged during the launch, and a 'sunshade' had to be improvised to prevent overheating. As with the crisis on Apollo 13 and some later demonstrations on the Shuttle, this sort of event shows how humans in space can overcome technical problems which would be very difficult or impossible with robots or unmanned craft. A similar problem was encountered by the Soviet cosmonauts in 1987 when they tried to dock Kvant, the rear-mounted astrophysics module, with their Mir complex. An 'extraneous object' lodged between Mir and the module, preventing a hermetic seal: cosmonauts Romanenko and Laveikin had to take a space walk in order to remove it.

So there has been Skylab, Salyut and Mir, and long before each of these was placed in orbit, the public knew how they would look from paintings. The same is true of the next stages, notably the International Space Station (ISS) now being planned by NASA with the European Space Agency (ESA), Canada and Japan. Part of Europe's contribution is the *Columbus* polar

Artist Profile

FRANK KELLY FREAS

Frank Kelly Freas was born in 1922 and lives in Los Angeles. He is a graduate of the Art Institute of Pittsburgh.

At the age of seven or eight he became interested in Buck Rogers, drawing that intrepid explorer's spaceships in kindergarten. He later admired the artwork of Virgil Finlay and Ed Cartier, and, in the astronomical field, Chesley Bonestell. His first professional work was in *Weird Tales*, November 1950. He considers himself to be 75 per cent illustrator, but also a fine artist and portraitist. Frank has worked for most major publishers of SF magazines and books, and is also the author of *Astounding Fifties, The Art of Science Fiction* (1977) and *A Separate Star* (1985). He has also done TV backgrounds, commercials and animations. His work is owned by Skylab crew-members (he designed their suit patch), authors Algis Budrys and the late Robert Heinlein, and NASA scientists.

However, from the point of view of this book, his most interesting work is perhaps the series of posters that he produced in the early 1970s. A visit to Cape Canaveral to witness the launch of Apollo 15 led, he says, to feelings of exaltation, awe, frustration and pale blue funk! The whole space programme was being cut back, slowed down — and this was a clear disaster. Mankind's destiny lay in space — his goal, his *Lebensraum*, his very salvation. Frank's answer was to produce a series of posters with slogans like 'We (still) have a choice?' (page 56), 'It takes ALL the little SYSTEMS to make the big ones GO!', or 'Er — suppose Isabella had said "NO"!' These were distributed to hundreds of schools, NASA used them in its own educational programme, and 50,000 science-fiction fans spread them throughout the country. He says that the letter file which resulted is pure inspiration to anyone who wonders about popular interest in space. The idea was not simply to spread the message, but to inspire and stimulate thought. And it did.

Left: 'Progress Supply Craft Makes Rendezvous with Salyut Space Station' by **Andrei Sokolov** (acrylics, 27½ × 19½ in/700 × 500 mm). The craft are docking above the Caspian Sea.
Right: 'Working in Space' by **Andrei Sokolov** (1986, acrylics, 21 × 23 in/530 × 584 mm). Solar panels are attached to Mir by cosmonauts Dzhanibekov and Savinykh (who visited Birmingham, England, in 1988).
Right, bottom: 'Sunrise', a sketch made by **Alexei Leonov** from personal experience (water-colour/tempera, 4¾ × 6¼ in/120 × 160 mm, all courtesy Space Art International).

Artist Profile

ALEXEI LEONOV

Alexei Arkhipovich Leonov was born on 30 May 1934 in Listvyanka, in the Kemerovo region of the USSR, the eighth of a family of nine. Upon finishing secondary school in Kaliningrad in 1953 he enrolled at the Academy of Arts in Riga. But almost immediately he left and entered the Chuguyev Air Force School, from which he graduated with honours in 1957. He qualified as a paradrop instructor in the Soviet Air Force, making over 100 drops himself. He joined the cosmonaut corps in 1960 and made no secret of the fact that his one ambition was to be the first man on the Moon. He is a Brigadier General, and currently Deputy Director of the Yuri Gagarin Cosmonaut Training Centre.

Alexei was the co-pilot of Voskhod 2, and was the first man to perform extravehicular activity (EVA), popularly known as 'walking in space', in March 1965. As a keen amateur artist he later painted his own self-portrait floating in space (something which turns most space artists green with envy). He was awarded the title 'Hero of the Soviet Union' and received the Order of Lenin. He was also command pilot for the Apollo-Soyuz Test Project in July 1975, and presented the Apollo astronauts with a unique gift — a portrait of each of them as sketched by himself in space.

After their meeting, Alexei was able to advise Andrei Sokolov (q.v.) on the accuracy of his work, and the two also collaborated on a large number of paintings, some of which toured the USA during the Apollo-Soyuz Test Project (ASTP). Alexei has written more than ten books on space, some of them for children. He has a great sense of humour.

Artist Profile

WAYNE BEGNAUD

Wayne Begnaud was born in 1955 and lives in Rialto, California. He is a graduate of the Art Center College of Design, Pasadena, with a Bachelor of Fine Art degree in illustration.

Watching the Apollo 8 mission in 1968 sparked a fascination with spaceflight that has grown stronger over the years. The first artist to inspire him was Robert McCall, and he first produced his own space art in 1969. He thinks of himself as 50 per cent illustrator, 50 per cent fine artist — with a desire to be 100 per cent fine artist. He works in gouache or acrylics, or sometimes in oils, and uses an airbrush.

Wayne helped to design the Apollo/Soyuz flight patch worn by the American astronauts and Soviet cosmonauts during the ASTP mission (which makes it appropriate that he should share this page with Leonov). He has worked as a freelance artist, but is currently with the Lockheed Corporation, producing many aviation-related illustrations.

He believes his art will only reach its greatest level of expression, unhindered by the constraints of the commercial art field, when he is able to concentrate on fine art, adding, 'No other subject excites, inspires or motivates me to create art like the subject of spaceflight'.

platform; its own shuttle, Hermes, is under development. More than ever, these stations will grow by accretion, and current designs already look very different from the wheels and spheres of the 1950s, consisting as they do of struts, girders, modules and solar 'wings' (which replace the earlier reflectors). Unfortunately, many of the illustrations which appear in books and magazines are credited merely 'Artist's rendering' or 'Photo courtesy NASA', with no indication of the name of the artist who has spent many long hours producing them. The reader may recognize some of those here. . .

The paintings on these pages are by the leading Soviet space artists. There are several other excellent space artists working in the USSR, but unfortunately difficulties in communication (in more ways than one) prevented them from being included here. Andrei Sokolov and Alexei Leonov have collaborated on many paintings, as well as producing individual works. But Leonov is the envy of all other space artists because he was once a cosmonaut; he made the first space walk in March 1965. Only astronaut/artist Alan Bean, who visited the Moon with Apollo 12, can compete with that.

'Hubble Space Telescope' by **Paul Hudson**
(acrylics, courtesy of the artist, © 1988
Thomasson-Grant, Inc.)

Above: A 1985 rendering of the Space Shuttle with early space station modules, painted by **Ed Valigursky** for Popular Mechanics (courtesy of the artist). Compare this with his 1950s version on page 18.
Right: **Jack Olson's** 'Space Station and Shuttle' (water-colour and tempera, 20 × 30 in/508 × 762 mm, courtesy Boeing Aerospace).

The Big Eye Paul Hudson's fine painting on pages 40–1 shows the event that has been long awaited by astronomers — the placing in Earth-orbit of the Hubble Space Telescope. It is named after the US astronomer Edwin P. Hubble, whose theory of the expanding universe was to have been one of the first items on the agenda for study when launched (originally scheduled for May 1986 on Shuttle *Atlantis*, but of course postponed because of the *Challenger* tragedy). The telescope, with its 94-inch/2.4-m mirror, is as high as a four-storey building, and will allow observers to see seven times further into space than ground-based telescopes. If it were turned upon Jupiter (not its intention), it should give a resolution comparable with the Voyager images. It has no thrusters to enable it to change altitude (gas molecules would affect observations), so it needs to be boosted periodically, using the Shuttle's robot arm, as its 400-mile/650-km orbit decays.

The basic Space Station, to be operating in the mid-1990s, has a rectangular structure to which various pressurized modules can be attached. Experiment modules from other countries, such as Japan, will also be added. An artist who has specialized in painting such structures because he was himself a Boeing engineer, is John (Jack) J. Olson, who is also a master photographer and a glider pilot. Oddly enough, Jack does not consider himself an artist and modestly 'never thought his work would have any value'. He says that he merely painted to illustrate his engineering designs; none the less, his superb work is in the Smithsonian Institution, and the examples here speak for themselves.

Artist Profile

JOHN J. OLSON

Jack Olson was born in 1922, and lives in Seattle, Washington. He obtained a BS degree at North Dakota State University (1940–42), an Industrial Design Certificate from Minneapolis College of Art and Design (1946–49), studied Aerospace Science at Washington University — the list goes on. He was a World War II pilot from 1942–46, and now enjoys gliding.

For 25 years Jack Olson was an engineer and preliminary concept designer for the Boeing Aerospace Company. In 1961 the graphics studio could not deliver in time, so he began to produce the artwork himself. This led to his producing dozens of highly accurate paintings of space stations, shuttlecraft and orbiting solar-power satellites, which have been reproduced in many books and magazines, in many countries.

His major work, he feels, is a painting entitled 'Space Solar Power Construction Facility', a masterpiece in technical drawing and perspective of which R.A. Smith would have heartily approved. This is one of 20 paintings now owned by the Smithsonian Institution in Washington, DC, an honour which Jack Olson says he never imagined would fall to him. Other examples of his work hang in the Museum of Flight, Seattle, and the Space Museum, Huntsville, Alabama.

JOHN OLSON 81

43

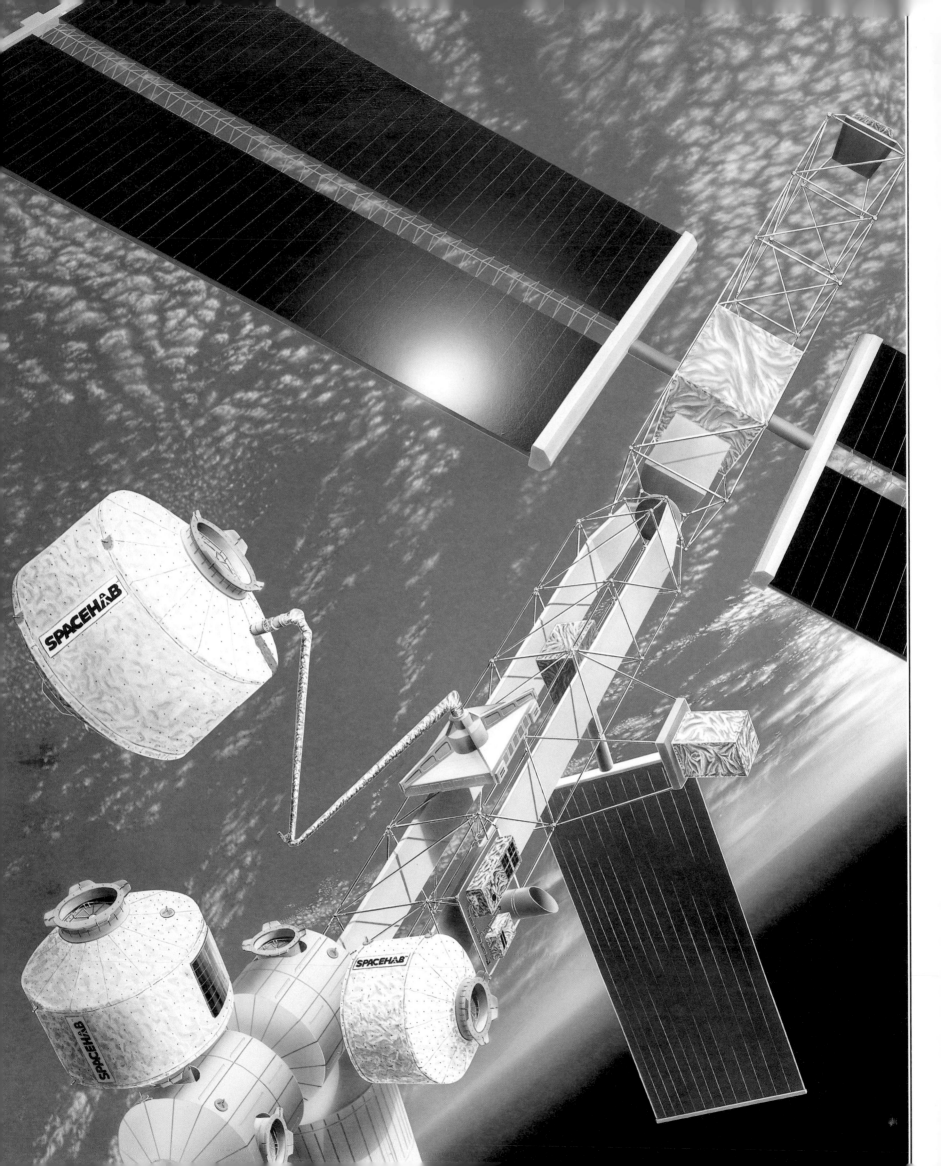

Left: 'Space Station A' by **Dennis Davidson** (acrylics, 35 × 54 in/890 × 1370 mm, courtesy of the artist, © 1986 Spacehab, Inc.) depicts Spacehab modules attached to the US/International Space Station. Right: 'Tin Can One' by **Mark Maxwell** (1986, acrylics on masonite, 8 × 15 in/203 × 381 mm, collection of Ken Moore, courtesy of the artist) shows his own hypothetical modular space station. (Pages 48–9) Two space station visions: (left) 'LEO Space Station' by **Carter Emmart** (1986, magic marker, 20 × 24 in/508 × 610 mm, courtesy of the artist). A cone-shaped Mars lander is next to a rectangular satellite hangar; (right) 'Translunar Pit Stop' by **Mark Dowman** (1988 acrylics, 21 × 14in/533 × 355 mm, © NASA).

Artist Profile

DENNIS M. DAVIDSON

Born in 1955, Dennis Davidson obtained a BA in biology in 1979 at the University of California, San Diego, and studied design and illustration at the Art Center School of Design, Pasadena, at Palomar College, San Marcos, and Mesa College, San Diego. He now lives in New York.

He started his career in space art in 1984 as Art Director for a NASA/CAL Space Summer Study: 'Space Resources 1985–2010'. Both contemporary space artists and commercial non-space artists have had an influence on his work. Producing both illustration and fine art, Dennis has contributed to books, including *Moonwalk* (1989) and the *Society of Illustrators' Annual*, 1988. He is particularly interested in depicting the Earth and the Moon in 'non-geocentred' orientation.

His major work to date is 'Above the Moon', a 30 × 34-in/76 × 86-cm painting in acrylics on canvas depicting the Earth, Moon and Sun in symbolic alignment. He is currently Astronomical Artist and Art Supervisor at the Hayden Planetarium in the American Museum of Natural History, New York City. His work was included in the exhibitions 'Art and the Cosmos', Lawrence Hall of Science (1986–87), IAAA/USSR Union of Scientists 'Art from Earth', Minsk, Kiev, Moscow, Los Angeles and San Diego (1989–90), and 'Man's Psychology in Space at the Beginning of the Cosmic Era', Moscow (spring 1989).

Artist Profile

MARK MAXWELL

Mark Craig Maxwell was born in 1960 and lives in Knoxville, Tennessee. He dropped out of high school to pursue a broadcasting degree, then dropped out of college to take up painting, in which he is self-taught.

He has had a lifelong interest in space and SF, having been born a couple of years after the start of the Space Age. Keeping up with the space programme introduced him to the imagery of various illustrators, and he was particularly impressed by Ed Valigursky. His interest in 'pure' space art became serious after buying *The Grand Tour* by Miller and Hartmann.

Mark's own first attempts at creating space art began at the age of 12 when he tried to paint his impression of a total lunar eclipse — in hideous fluorescent temperas on a piece of black poster board. His work was first published in *Meteorites and Their Parent Planets* (1987). Since then it has appeared in *Beyond Gravity* (1988), the Asimov 'Library of the Universe' series, *Omni* magazine, publications by the National Space Society, and many other places. He is currently engaged in pre-production work for a film entitled *Spirit*, and has also completed a large, detailed rendering of a proposed futuristic theme-park complex. He has exhibited at three World SF Conventions and produces a lot of SF, as well as technical and industrial illustration. Shuttle astronaut Charles Walker owns one of Mark's paintings of a space station. Having just acquired a large telescope, Mark hopes to learn more about astronomy — and art.

'Astronaut Montage' by **Wayne Begnaud** (oils, 32 × 18 in/813 ×
457 mm, courtesy of the artist) depicts the historic missions of astronaut
Vance Brand, who served on the Apollo-Soyuz test project in July 1975,

as commander on Shuttle STS–5 in November 1982, and made the first untethered space walk using the MMU in February 1984 during the STS–41B mission.

Ultimately, it is essential that space must pay its way. Among the new facilities at the Space Station, therefore, will be commercially-owned and -operated modules. These include Spacehab and an Industrial Space Facility (ISF). On page 44 Dennis Davidson illustrates the design by Spacehab, Inc., of Seattle, Washington, based on the 1986 configuration of the ISS. The small Spacehab modules were designed to be interchangeable, multi-use units and as habitat/experimental extensions for the Shuttle — for example, for bio-medical research requiring quarantine. When in the Shuttle's cargo bay, Spacehab's flat 'roof' would allow astronauts a clear view to the rest of the cargo bay, unlike ESA's cylindrical Spacelab; experiments requiring exposure to vacuum could also be mounted there.

Although the emphasis here is, not surprisingly, on Western proposals, it should not be forgotten that the Soviet Union has had its own small space station operating continuously in orbit for years. The industrialization of space is likely to benefit the Soviet Union earlier than Western nations, and probably to a greater extent. The Japanese space programme, already comparable with the European one in size, is also expanding fast.

Artist Profile

MARK DOWMAN

Born in 1961, Mark Dowman attended the Glassell School of Art, Houston Museum of Fine Arts (1978) and now lives in Houston, Texas.

His influences include Syd Mead, Robert McCall and Jim Burns, as well as *Monty Python* animator Terry Gilliam. His first published work was for an advanced propulsion project for NASA in 1979, and he considers himself both an illustrator and fine artist. His work appears in *Pioneering the Space Frontier* (1986), the *Omni Space Almanac* (1987) and Asimov's 'Library of the Universe' series, as well as various international publications. It has been used on TV in *Nova* and newscasts.

Mark is now part of the Eagle Visuals team, under the direction of Pat Rawlings with John Lowery, Mike Stovall and Doug McLeod, producing work which may be solo or collaborative. He has exhibited at the Aspen Design Conference (1980), 'Other Worlds' (IAAA: 1985–88) and 'Pioneering the Space Frontier' (1988). He also paints SF and fantasy subjects, and his skills include model-building, photography and computer graphics.

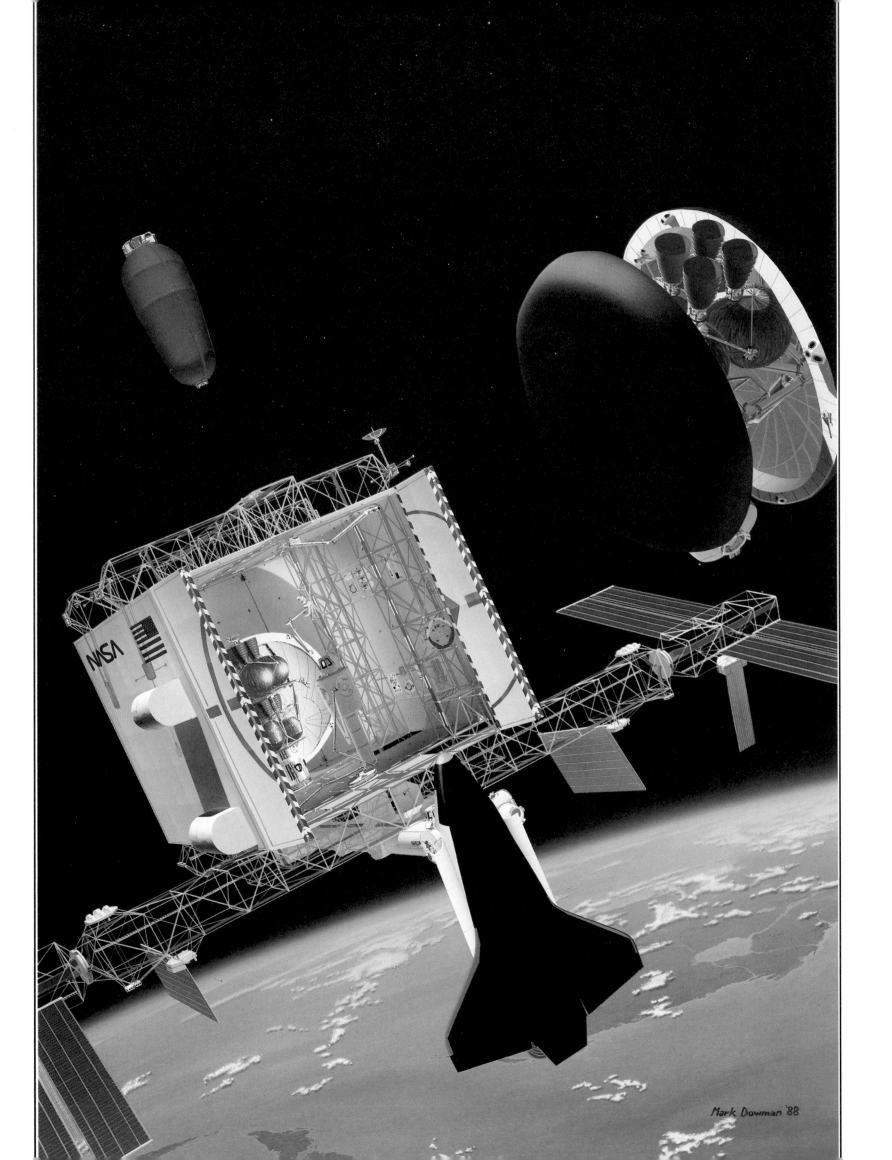

Mark Dowman '88

DOUG MCLEOD © 1988

51

Wayne Begnaud

Reinventing the Wheel The idea of a wheel-shaped space station is far from dead; it has actually grown. When space tourism becomes a reality, artificially-created gravity may be a necessity (away from the zero-gravity games areas!), and the only way known to do this at present is to rotate the station. So future space stations may well resemble the giant constructions on these and the two previous pages.

The most grandiose proposals of all originated in a freshman course in physics at Princeton University in 1969 — the year in which men landed on the Moon. Dr Gerard K. O'Neill posed the question, 'Is the surface of a planet really the right place for an expanding technological civilization?'

Artist Profile

PIERRE MION

Pierre Mion was born in Bryn Mawr, Pennsylvania, in 1931, and now lives in Lovettsville, Virginia. He attended the George Washington University and studied with Elliot O'Hara at the Corcoran School of Art.

He did space drawings as a child, and since 1961 has produced space art for *National Geographic Magazine*, *Look* magazine and *Air & Space*, and has produced murals for the Smithsonian. He estimates that he is two-thirds illustrator, one-third fine artist. He has also designed stamps for the US Postal Service. Places that have exhibited his work or hold examples of it include the

National Air and Space Museum, Hayden Planetarium, the Society of Illustrators (New York) and the Mitsukoshi Gallery, Tokyo. His work is owned by Senator Barry Goldwater, Apollo astronauts Michael Collins and David Scott, and Norman Rockwell, among others.

Pierre has many interests other than space art. In addition to painting portraits, animals, aircraft, transportation, oceanographic and geological subjects, he has had a parallel career as a driver of racing cars and motor cycles, from 1950 to 1966, and was National Champion in sports cars in 1959 and 1961. He flies gliders, rides horses, scuba dives and skis, restored the old farmhouse where he now lives, and says that he will continue painting until he drops. It could be said that he is a man of many worlds.

Using material from the Moon or asteroids, the results looked like inside-out, artificial planets, cylinders — or giant wheels. By 1975 the preferred design was the Stanford Torus — an immense inner-tube shape, 390 ft/120 m wide and some 4 miles/6.5 km in circumference. It had a central hub with a contra-rotating docking area. This would be home for 10,000 people, with recreation and industrial areas, lakes and everything necessary for a healthy life. The most likely location for such a station is the 'L−5 libration point', one of two points which lie at equal distances from the Earth and the Moon. Consequently, it became known as an L−5 Colony, giving rise to the L−5 Society (now incorporated in the US-based National Space Society).

Back to the Moon
The Next Small Step for Man

4

Apollo was a technological dead-end. Twelve men went to the Moon and back in totally expendable vehicles, but no one built upon that achievement. This was quite different from the visions of von Braun and the other visionaries of the 1950s, who expected that men and women would return time and again to the Moon, building larger and more sophisticated bases, until they even became self-supporting. O'Neill and his supporters prefer man-made worlds, but even they require a presence on the Moon to operate the mass-drivers which would deliver material to build the colonies. The Shuttle and space stations are a new start.

(Pages 50–1) 'Cyclops' by **Doug Mcleod** (1988, acrylics, 14 × 19in/355 × 482 mm, courtesy of the artist) is a large, extended version of the wheel space station, spinning for artificial gravity and with a hub for docking.
(Page 52) 'Orbiting Space Complex' by **Wayne Begnaud** (gouache, 17 × 16 in/432 × 406 mm, courtesy of the artist) is a fourth- or fifth-generation space station, also wheel-shaped, 50 or 60 years from now — a time when access to Earth orbit will be considered routine.
(Page 53) **Pierre Mion's** visualization of an L–5 Colony (gouache, 15¾ × 16½ in/400 × 420 mm, © 1976 National Geographic Society), perhaps the grandest concept yet for a space station.

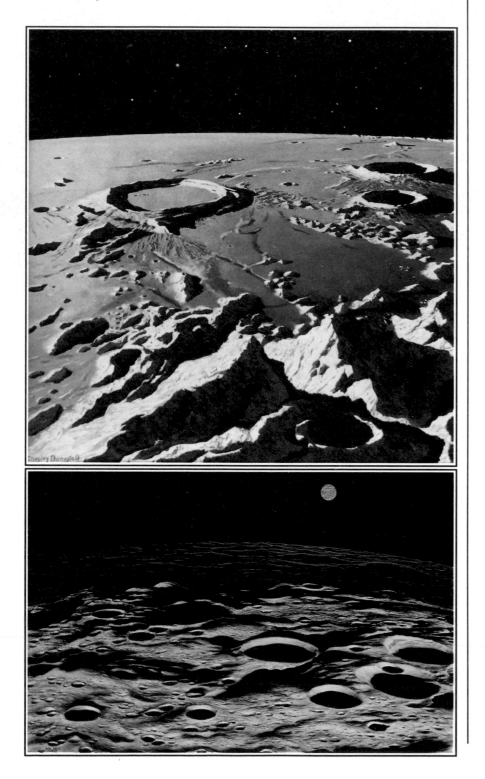

Left, top: 'The Moon's Apennines', a view from orbit by **Chesley Bonestell**.
Left, bottom: 'The Moon's South Pole' by **Don Davis**, with Earth on the horizon. Parts of the Moon's polar areas never receive sunlight, and are the most likely sites for (frozen) water to be found. (Courtesy of the artist)

Artist Profile

DONALD E. DAVIS

Don Davis was born in 1952 in Oakland, California, and now lives in Salt Lake City, Utah. He attended Ravenswood and Menlo Atherton High School, graduating in 1970.

In 1968 he had began working for the US Geological Survey's branch of Astrogeological Studies, where he learned about the surfaces of the Moon and other planets. While there he painted a pair of maps, recreating the Moon's appearance during its early development. In particular, his work dealt with impact cratering mechanics and how they shaped the surfaces of the inner planets in the distant past.

When the decline of the US Planetary Exploration Program caused funding for his job to be cut back he turned to freelance work, including book and magazine illustration. Among others, his work appears in such books as *Solar System* (1985), Sagan's *Cosmos* (1980) and *Comet* (1985), as well as the cover for Sagan's Pulitzer Prize-winning book *The Dragons of Eden* (1977), the US paperback edition of O'Neill's *The High Frontier* (1977), and *The New Solar System* (1981).

From 1979 Don produced a number of model globes, commencing with surface models of Venus and Mars for the *Cosmos* TV series. He won an Emmy for his efforts, and was also nominated for an Emmy for his work on the later TV *Planet Earth* series, for which he sculpted an Earth globe including ocean-bottom details, other globes of Earth in space, and two complex animation sequences of impact events. He is now employed at the Hansen Planetarium at Salt Lake City, utilizing the Digistar computer graphic star projection system, one of the most advanced in the world.

Above: 'Alien Space Probe Enters the Earth-Moon System' by **Frank Kelly Freas** (1975, acrylics, 15 × 20 in/380 × 508 mm, interior for Analog, courtesy of the artist). Earth eclipses the Sun, whose corona is visible. (It is interesting to compare this with Ron Miller's on page 126, which shows one of our star probes leaving the Solar System ...)

In her 1987 report to NASA, 'Leadership and America's Future in Space', astronaut Sally Ride recommended a new Office of Exploration. The report suggested four initiatives: the use of space age technology to better understand our home planet, the exploration of the Solar System by automated spacecraft, the establishment of a permanent lunar base, and a manned mission to Mars.

There has since been some discussion between scientists (and artists) on whether we should concentrate on Mars, and whether the Moon would merely form an obstacle on the road to that fascinating planet. Some, such as Dr Isaac Asimov, have made a case for the idea that a Moon base is the next essential step, and that the inhabitants of a lunar base might be the people best suited to lead us to Mars. Others begrudge the time and resources (out of annual budgets) that going back to the Moon would require.

On balance, the experience and advances in technology (such as closed-cycle life-support systems) which would result from the establishment of a base on the airless Moon would probably benefit a later expedition to explore thin-aired Mars. And work on plans for a lunar base could begin immediately, with the aim of implementing them within a decade or so. By that time — the early 2000s — scientists should probably have obtained sufficient information to plan manned Mars missions with a good chance of success.

The paintings on the next few pages show how artists have interpreted the plans of scientists for a return to our nearest neighbour in space.

Left, top: 'We (still) have a choice?', one of a series of posters by **Frank Kelly Freas** to promote the Apollo programme (courtesy of the artist).
Left, centre: 'Apollo 12' by **Pierre Mion** (oils, 38 × 60 in/965 × 1524 mm, courtesy of the artist) shows how astronauts Conrad and Bean (also an artist) landed close to the Surveyor 3 probe in November 1969.
Left, bottom: 'Crisis on Apollo 13' by **Mark Paternostro** (acrylics, courtesy of the artist) depicts the moment when, in April 1970, astronaut Lovell radioed to Houston, 'Hey — we've got a problem here!', making it the most tense of all missions.

Right, top: 'Moon Mining' by **Pierre Mion** (gouache, 15¾ × 21 in/ 400 × 533 mm, © 1976 National Geographic Society) shows the lunar base with an electromagnetic mass driver which propels lunar materials into space to build the L−5 Colonies.
Right, centre: 'Survey Team' by **Julian Baum** (photograph, using models and painting technique, courtesy of the artist) depicts astronauts using metal detectors near their base.
Right, bottom: 'When I Was a Kid ...' by **Pat Rawlings** (acrylics, 15 × 27 in/380 × 686 mm, © 1985 Lunar and Planetary Institute). Man and child sit by the site of the future Apollo Museum; on the left is an old, buried lunar base and a mass driver. (Note the logo of the National Air and Space Museum, which owns all Apollo artefacts left on the Moon.)

Artist Profile

MARK PATERNOSTRO

Mark Paternostro was born in 1952. He attended the University of Wisconsin at Madison from 1970 to 1973, and at Milwaukee from 1975 to 1976, obtaining a fine arts degree in illustration and communication arts. He was an instructor at Milwaukee Institute of Art and Design from 1984 to 1985, and now lives in Chicago.

In 1975, while being interviewed for a position at Grafilm Inc. in Milwaukee, Mark first saw *Astronomy* magazine, for which Grafilm did the typesetting. Next day he contacted Stephen A. Walther (now unfortunately deceased), *Astronomy*'s founder and a lover of space art. Mark was given a test assignment and his work first appeared in the March 1976 issue. Later he became staff artist. He says that Steve Walther and Adolph Schaller imprinted 'the look' that still stands today.

His work has appeared in several publications, including *The New Astronomy*, Encyclopaedia Britannica's *Science and Future Annual, Comet* (1985), Asimov's 'Library of the Universe' series and the Raintree *Encyclopedia of Science* (1984). It has also appeared on TV in *Milwaukee Profiles, Nightline* and *Nova* for the Public Broadcasting Service (PBS). Since 1985 Mark has worked as Astronomical Artist and Visual Designer at the Adler Planetarium, Chicago; he considers his major work to be the 'Future Feedback Network' exhibit and performance, and 'Quest for Infinity/The New Universe'. He also paints SF and other subjects, believing that 'it is the action of creation itself that is the essence of art. Types, genres, styles are there for the taking or to leave.'

(Pages 58–9) *A future Lunar Landing Vehicle (LLV) painted by* **Paul Hudson** *(acrylics, courtesy of the artist, © 1988 Thomasson-Grant, Inc.) This will be the workhorse that links craft in lunar orbit with base camps and suchlike on the surface.*

Artist Profile

PAT RAWLINGS

Born in 1955, Pat Rawlings has a BA in applied design and visual arts from the University of Houston at Clear Lake, Texas.

In 1978, while working for a NASA contractor, he was exposed to space art in NASA publications, and met Bob McCall, who was painting a mural at Johnson Space Center (JSC). His own work first appeared in *New Earths* (1981). He considers himself 90 per cent illustrator, 10 per cent fine artist.

Pat has become a leading exponent of 'hard' space art, specializing in vehicles, lunar bases and space stations, but feels his major work to be 'Space Station over the Terminator' and 'First Light' (not a hardware painting) for the NASA Office of Exploration. He has contributed to many books, including *Welcome to Mars* by Ben Bova (who also owns his work), *The Universe* (1987) and *Discover: The World of Science*, as well as a TV series about a lunar base. He has also done pre-production art for Walt Disney Studios and ABC.

His work was included in the IAAA exhibition 'Other Worlds', and his one-man show '2069' was held at JSC. Pat Rawlings is Art Director at Eagle Visuals, a department of Eagle Engineering/Eagle Aerospace of Houston, Texas, providing visualizations of future space concepts in everything from line to airbrush. He says that he wants to make space and its trappings less intimidating to non-scientific people by including human interest without sacrificing technical content.

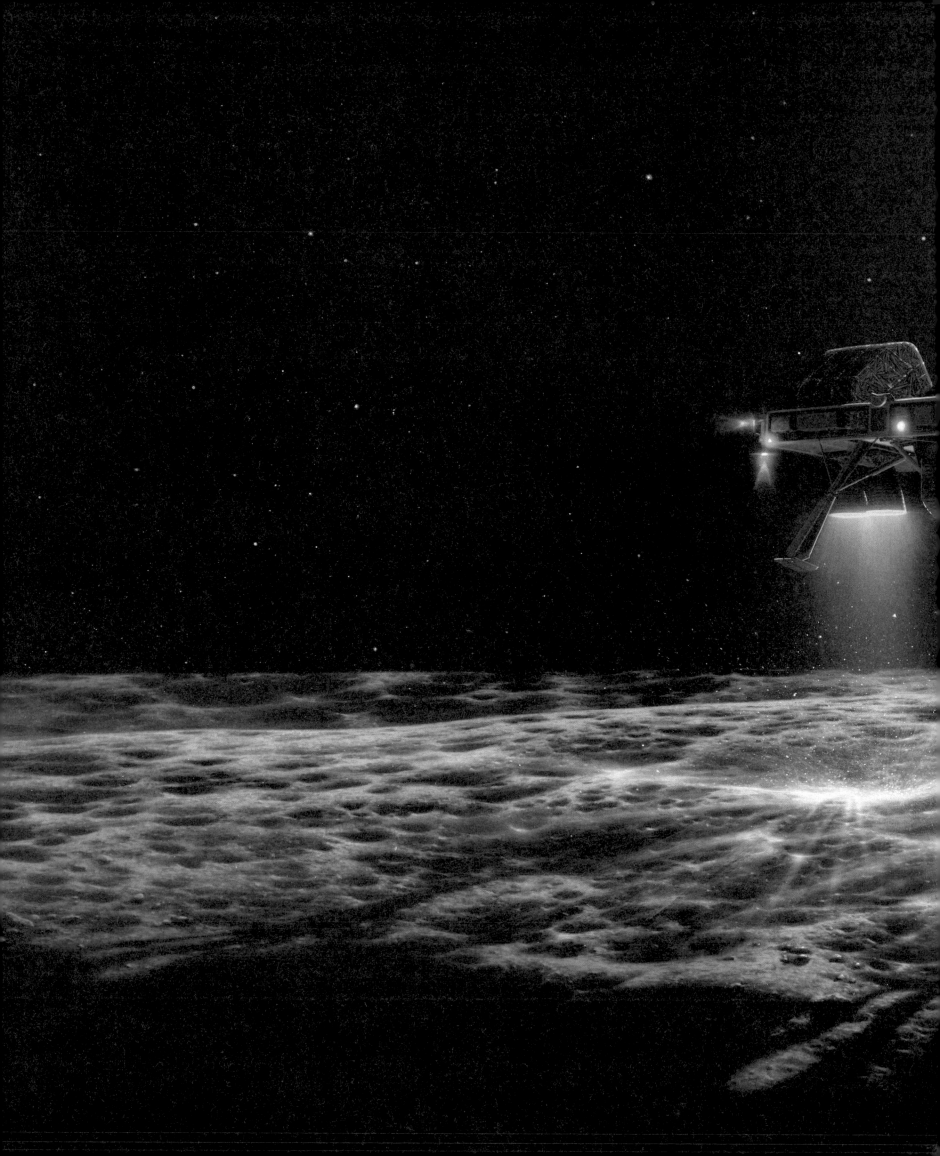

Lunar Bases While the Soviets are certainly pushing ahead with a reinvigorated programme of Mars exploration, they also have plans to return to the Moon. Robotic surface explorers would be followed, this time, by humans and finally a manned base. An *international* Moon colony would, of course, be even more desirable, so it is encouraging that NASA Administrator, Dr James C. Fletcher, favours this view.

On pages 64–5 Pat Rawlings depicts the new-style lunar module which could form the workhorse for the early lunar base. A flexible tube enables crew to transfer into a roving vehicle, at lower right. Above, in Jack Olson's painting, pressurized living quarters are being covered in lunar 'soil' as protection against radiation, extremes of temperature and micrometeorites. Indeed, many years ago Dr D.J. Sheppard of the BIS suggested that the best way of constructing a lunar base might be to tunnel into the granitic highlands.

Further calculations intended to discover the amount of room available for lunar colonies gave a rather mind-boggling answer. If our descendants decided to honeycomb only one per cent of the volume of rock available at a maximum depth of 12 miles/20 km (the equivalent of our deepest mines, in the one-sixth lunar gravity), a total floor area of 1370 miles/2200 km at normal room height would be available. This would equal several million L–5-type colonies! An extreme example, perhaps, but there are several factors in favour of underground bases. Any type or scale of tunnelling will

Above, left: 'Moon Base' by **Jack Olson** (water-colour and tempera, 20 × 30 in/508 × 762 mm, courtesy Boeing Aerospace and the artist) shows a lunar base being covered in lunar 'soil' for radiation protection. Above, right: 'Mining Operations on the Moon' by **Paul DiMare** (gouache, 20½ × 14½ in/520 × 368 mm, courtesy of the artist) — a vista from a low hill, showing a roving vehicle returning to its base camp, having completed its four-lunar day cycle (56 Earth days) expedition to the polar region. The operations base itself is on the distant lunar plain.

(Pages 60–1) 'Lunar Outpost' by **Dennis Davidson** (acrylics, 24 × 35 in/610 × 890 mm, courtesy of the artist) was painted for a NASA/California Space Institute summer study, 'Space Resources 1984–2010' in 1985. It shows an advanced lunar facility for extracting oxygen powered by solar furnaces (right). A six-wheeled lunar excursion vehicle (LEV) in the foreground is derived from the Apollo Lunar Rover; a lunar tug delivers liquid oxygen to lunar orbit.
(Pages 64–5) 'Unloading at Pad 3' by **Pat Rawlings** (acrylics, 18 × 27 in/457 × 686 mm, © Eagle Engineering for NASA/Johnson Space Center) illustrates the variety of items necessary to service a re-usable lunar lander. These include a pressurized surface vehicle, a crane, a flexible pressurized tunnel, a fuel tanker, an auxiliary power cart and a replacement engine.

Artist Profile

PAUL DIMARE

Paul DiMare was born in 1959, attended the Cooper School of Art, took commercial art in high school, and had a three-year apprenticeship at Katzan Studios. His first influences were Ludek Pesek and Bob McCall.

He produced his first space art in 1977, thinks of himself purely as an illustrator, and his first published work was a cover for *Astronomy* in September 1985. Since then his work has appeared on, or in, *Astronomy*, *Sky and Telescope* and *Space World* magazine, *Exploring Your Solar System* and the Asimov 'Library of the Universe' series. His major work to date is a Mars Base for the National Geographic Society (which he completed just before he sent these details). He prefers gouache used transparently, and employs an airbrush when necessary.

Paul is co-owner of a commercial studio in Cleveland, Ohio, providing editorial material and commercial art to a wide range of corporate clients. His work is owned by William K. Hartmann, who, he says, is also a big influence. He intends to develop as an artist, tries to make his scenes believable (the 'you are there' approach), and 'have fun with strong contrasts in space, light and dark, soft and hard textures, and lots of detail'. He is also an amateur astronomer and photographer, and tries to capture the elusive faint nebulae (see page 142) on film.

almost certainly have been tried and tested on Earth, and its cost could be as little as one-fiftieth that of surface constructions. Also, it should last virtually for ever; after all, limestone caves on Earth have survived for thousands of years. But from the artist's point of view a surface base will always win, as an underground base will look like little more than a low hill from above ground.

There is, however, one unquantifiable problem in lunar colonization, which only time and experience might resolve. Sunlight could be ducted in from the surface, where solar panels would provide power. But humans might not be able to live happily without windows through which to gaze at the lunar landscape, their blue home planet and the stars. An experienced submariner has been heard to comment that he would happily swap places with an astronaut on his way to Mars because at least the space traveller could look out of his porthole.

One thing is certain: whether constructed on the surface or underground, if a base is to develop into a city, it must be a place in which people will *want* to live — bright, spacious, with trees and gardens, vegetables and flowers; not cramped (although the early bases will surely be so), spartan, sterile and unwelcoming. Artists and designers should be in demand, as much as engineers. From the point of view of the industrialist, the Moon offers metallic minerals, oxygen, free vacuum, solar energy and a virtually infinite 'sink' for waste heat.

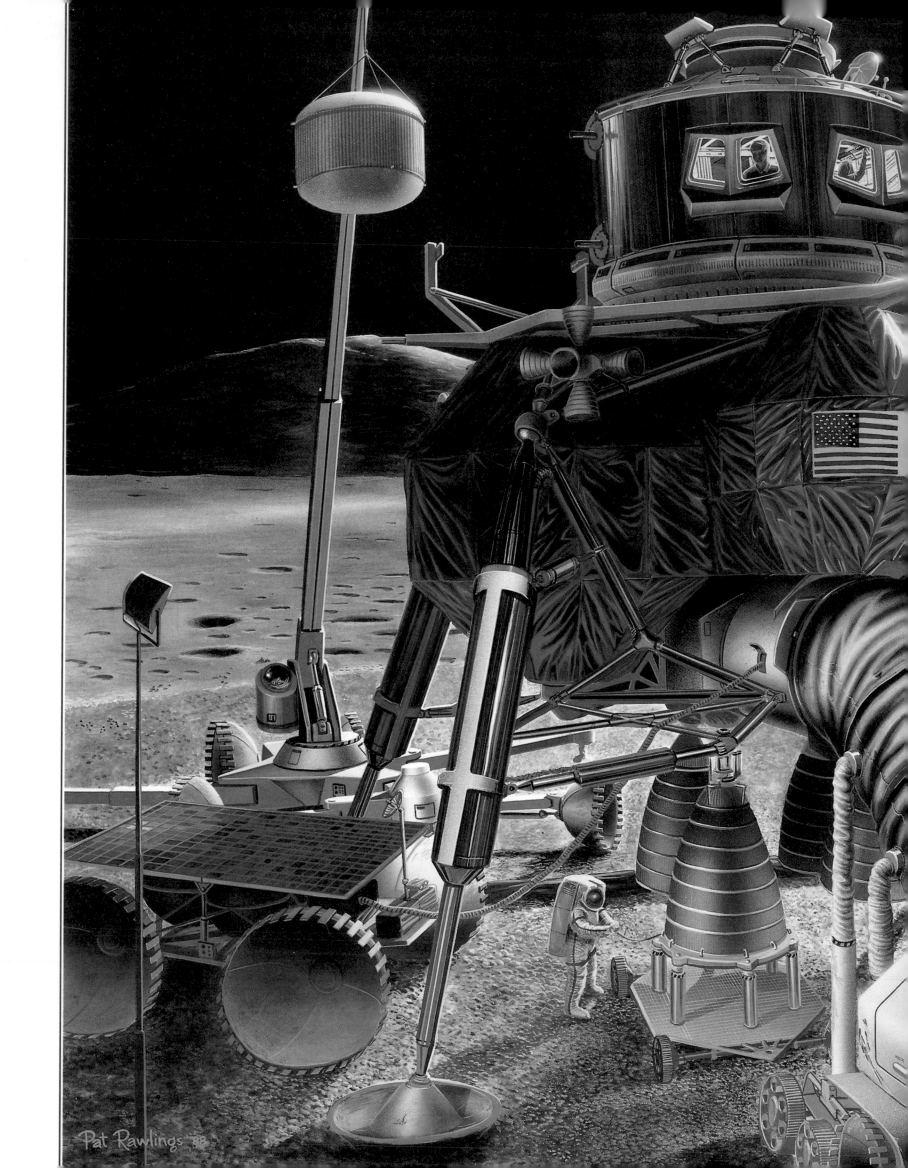

Pat Rawlings '88

The Solar System

From Past to Future

5

Some space artists specialize in painting future vehicles and bases, but almost all are fascinated by the idea of going back to the beginning of the universe: great swirling gas and dust clouds, glowing protostars bursting into nuclear flame and blasting the primordial atmospheres from their new-born planets — who could fail to be inspired by such cosmic spectacle?

The next few pages show how several artists have seen these sights in their imagination. We see planetesimals orbiting their dusty protosun, colliding with each other and either shattering or fusing together, gradually forming protoplanets. Our own Earth originated in just this way, and our bodies contain the atoms and molecules from the exploding supernovae which triggered the process. Smaller bodies bombard the early Earth and Moon, leaving the craters which we still see today on the Moon and many other planets and satellites, while erosion by weather, water and volcanic eruptions have concealed most of the evidence on Earth.

Life evolved more than three billion years ago. The portrayal of prehistoric scenes and animals is, in a sense, a sub-division of space art; Dorothy Sigler has painted many such subjects, as I have myself, but artists such as the Czechoslovakian Zdeněk Burian and, more recently, John Sibbick, are true specialists and produce reconstructions of prehistoric Earth and its life just as convincing as any scene on Mars in this book.

(Pages 66–7) 'Lunar Base During an Eclipse' by **William K. Hartmann** *(acrylics, from* Out of the Cradle, *1984, courtesy of the artist). On the night side of Earth observers see a lunar eclipse; inhabitants of the Moon-base are plunged into a coppery twilight for over an hour. Earth hangs low over this base in the impact basin Mare Orientale. Most of the base consists of modules heaped with protective soil; the solar panels (left) are briefly useless.*
Below: 'Protoplanet' by **Hans Martens** *(gouache, 12 × 16 ½in/300 × 420 mm, courtesy of the artist) — a scene which may have existed over 4500 million years ago, when the brand new planet Earth was starting to exist near its brand new Sun.*

Right: Three scenes in the Early Solar System by **Dorothy Sigler Norton** *(top),* **William Hartmann** *(centre) and* **Hans Martens** *(bottom). The top scene is somewhere between Venus and Earth, where silicate bodies are accreting until they reach 60 miles/100 km across. Some collide (centre) and stick together; finally they form planets — here, Earth and Moon (bottom).*

Artist Profile

DON DIXON

Don Dixon was born in 1951 and studied at Victor Valley College and the University of California at Berkeley, majoring in mathematics, physics and astronomy. He lives at Santa Ana, California.

He has been a freelance illustrator since 1972 and his early work as a space artist was strongly influenced by Bonestell. He is one of a few artists (including one Briton) to carry on the tradition started by Bonestell of having purely astronomical art on the cover of *The Magazine of Fantasy & Science Fiction*. His work also became widely known through the sets of slides which are marketed under the trade name 'Dixon Spacescapes', and used by educational institutions, planetariums and private collectors.

Don's work has appeared in the magazines *Astronomy, Starlog, Science Digest, Omni, Sky and Telescope, Technology Review* and several others. He has also contributed to many books, both as a space artist and SF cover artist. These include two books by T.A. Heppenheimer, *Colonies in Space* (1978) and *Toward Distant Suns* (1979), as well as *Exploring Our Solar System, Cosmos* (1980), *Comet* (1985), *The Macmillan Book of Astronomy* (1986) and *World Book Encyclopedia* (1986). (For the record, the painting of the double star Beta Lyrae in some editions of *Cosmos* credited to David A. Hardy is actually by Don Dixon. But then, Don admits that *Challenge of the Stars* made him take up the airbrush.)

His film and TV work includes special effects storyboard for *Airplane*, pre-production design for *Battle Beyond the Stars*, background art for *Cosmos* (KCET TV) and *Spaceships of the Mind* (BBC TV), and animation art for *Probing the Clouds of Venus* and *Jupiter Odyssey* (both NASA). He designed the NASA logo for the first reconnaissance of Saturn, and awards include one from NASA for his Venus animation, and a Certificate of Merit from the New York Society of Illustrators (1980). His work is owned by Ray Bradbury, Larry Niven, Kansas City Museum and the Adler Planetarium, Chicago.

Artist Profile

HANS MARTENS

Hans Martens was born in 1948 and educated at the Royal Academy of Art in The Hague, Netherlands, where he studied graphic design from 1964 to 1972. He also lives in The Hague.

His interest in space started when he was seven years old and saw the first article illustrated by Ludek Pesek in the *National Geographic Magazine* (see page 88). Pesek later criticized (kindly) Martens's work, which first appeared professionally in 1976, in a book by Chriet Titulaer entitled *The Great Book of Planets*, and has since appeared in the German magazine *PM*, *Omni* and the *Future* Calendar, 1981. He currently works as a graphic designer for the Royal Dutch Touring Club — a sister-club to the British Automobile Association.

Hans works mainly in gouache, using brush and airbrush, and has taken part in several exhibitions to promote the popular scientific magazine *Kijk*, for which he has worked for over 12 years. His work has also been exhibited in Antwerp, Belgium and at 'Space '86' in Utrecht, an exhibition which included the work of several Dutch artists (plus Peter Coene's 'IRAS' project, page 137) and other artists in this book, including Bonestell, Davis, Hardy, Hartmann, Lee, Leonov, McCall, Miller, Mion, Papanicolaou, Pesek and Sokolov, as well as Alan Bean.

His ambition is to produce a book of space paintings.

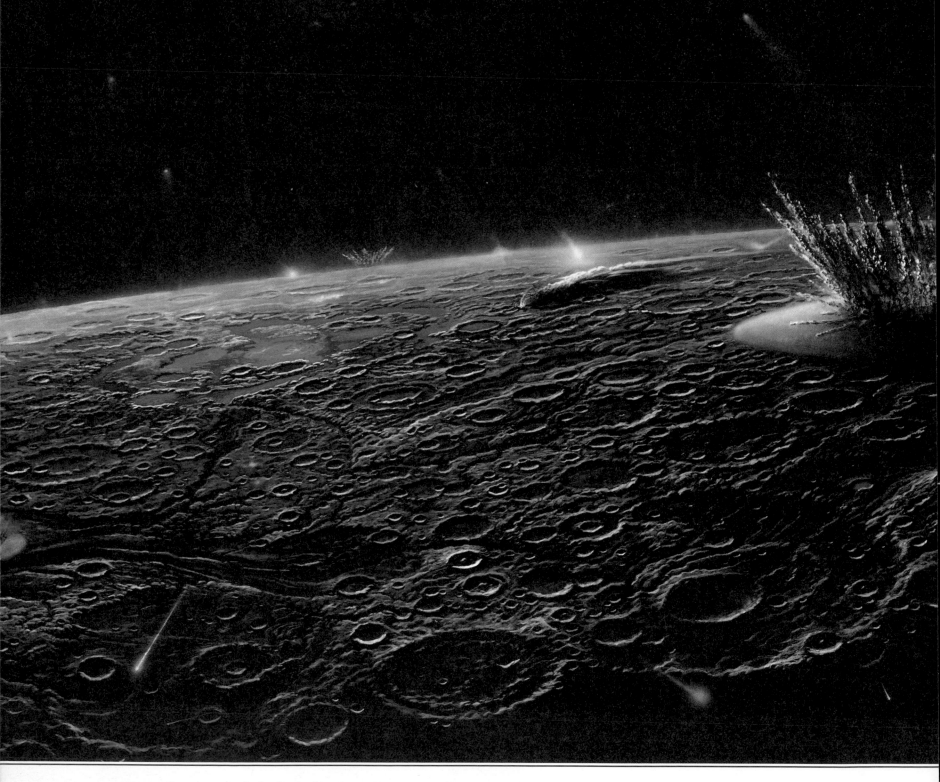

Bonestell was particularly fond of 'early Earth' scenes. Shortly after the *Collier's* articles appeared he was asked by *Life* magazine to illustrate the opening and closing articles in a new series, 'The World We Live In'. Bonestell and science editor Warren Young worked out a series of pictures from the primordial nebula to the end of the world. It was at this point that Bonestell had problems with *Life*. He sent them a spread showing the Earth glowing red-hot, its Sun having become a nova. Streams of lava flowed into

Above: 'Giant Impact on Early Earth' by **Adolf Schaller** (acrylics, 20 × 30 in/508 × 762 mm, courtesy of the artist) shows the 'era of bombardment' which existed 1.5 billion years ago as the planets swept up the remaining planetoids. Here a giant comet strikes the surface of the primitive Earth (its newly-formed moon in the sky), bringing its precious cargo of water to help create Earth's primordial oceans. The Moon retains the record, in its craters.

a valley, and on a ridge he showed a melting observatory with the corpses of astronomers clinging to rocks in the foreground.

The painting was returned with instructions to remove the observatory and skeletons. Bonestell promptly made a copy without them, which satisfied the queasy editors. The original version finished up at the Boston Museum of Science. Bonestell also had a penchant for destroying the Earth by giant meteorites or the like. His work is collected in *Worlds Beyond: The Art of Chesley Bonestell* (1983).

Above, top: 'Late Impact on the Forming Earth' by **Don Dixon**
(1988, acrylics, 11 × 16 in/280 × 406 mm, for the magazine National Geographic World, *courtesy of the artist) also shows a view from space of the late stage of bombardment.*
Right: *An oil painting by* **Chesley Bonestell** *showing the titanic impact which probably created the Moon's huge Mare Imbrium basin. (Courtesy Space Art International)*

'Atmosphere' by **Joe Tucciarone** (acrylics on canvas board, 23½ × 28 in/600 × 711 mm, courtesy of the artist) depicts the surface of the Earth soon after the crust cooled and the atmosphere formed. The young, close Moon hangs nearby. Meteors still enter the atmosphere and volcanoes erupt; life is still distant.

Left: 'Mayan Indians Worship an Eclipse' by **Mark Paternostro** (acrylics, courtesy of the artist). Mayan priests had a good knowledge of astronomy, and prepared tables by means of which they could predict eclipses. Even so, the disappearance of the source of all light and heat must have been a traumatic experience for the masses.

Right, top: A matt painting of the tiny, Moon-like planet Mercury by **Larry Ortiz** (acrylics, 12 × 15 in/305 × 380 mm, courtesy of the artist).

Right: In **William K. Hartmann's** painting (acrylics, 20 × 16 in/ 508 × 406 mm) the Sun's glare is blocked by a huge boulder on the rim of a crater, allowing the streamers of the corona and zodiacal light to become visible. The two 'stars' at top right are Venus and the Earth. (Acrylics, from The Grand Tour, 1981, courtesy of the artist.)

Artist Profile

WILLIAM K. HARTMANN

Bill Hartmann was born in 1939, making him, he says, 'not as old as some' — a reference to his surprise when he discovered that he had not been around in space art for as long as the writer of this book! He makes up for this in qualifications: a BS in physics, an MS in geology and a PhD in astronomy. He lives in Tucson, Arizona.

His grandfather was a painter who left Switzerland for the USA as a young man. As a boy, Bill pored over Bonestell's articles and books, first producing his own space art as a teenager, and first being published when in his thirties (in articles and textbooks, as well as Ron Miller's *Space Art*, for which he also wrote a foreword). He sees no conflict between fine art and illustration, as he approaches it, so considers his work 65 per cent fine art and 35 per cent illustration.

He co-authored and co-illustrated *Grand Tour, Out of the Cradle* and *Cycles of Fire*, and considers these to be his major works to date. He has also written and illustrated numerous articles, and has produced two college textbooks in multiple editions.

Bill's work was exhibited at a Planetary Society exhibition at Pasadena during a Voyager encounter, and in IAAA travelling exhibitions, including the current international one. His short story 'Handprints on the Moon' was included in *The Planets* (1985), a book which also included some interesting space art. His work is owned by Sokolov and other artists, as well as André Brahic of the Observatory of Paris, who specializes in Saturn's rings, and Robert A. Brown of the American Astronomical Society. He wants to work towards 'more international collaboration in space art so as to promote more general awareness of exploration as a mutually shared human adventure'.

Solar Fires By the time of the scene by Mark Paternostro, opposite, Man has been evolving for several million years and is worshipping one of the most awesome spectacles in nature — a solar eclipse. It is only at such a time that the pearly wings of the Sun's corona become visible. The Sun is, of course, a very ordinary star, smaller than some and larger than others; but because it is the centre of our planetary system and the source of all our light and energy it is of vital importance.

The closest planet to the Sun is tiny Mercury, with a day temperature of 427°C. Although only the vaguest markings are visible through a telescope, Bonestell predicted that it would be Moon-like, with craters. Mariner 10 images subsequently proved it to be very similar to the Moon in appearance.

The Veiled World When Lucien Rudaux illustrated his book *Sur les autres mondes* in the early 1930s (and for some decades afterwards), he could paint these two alternative views of the surface of the planet that is almost Earth's twin in size. Telescopically, Venus presents a bland, white face, and no astronomer could know what lay below its cloud banks until the introduction of radar and space probes. Spectroscopes showed no water vapour, so the clouds did not appear to be like Earth's, but it was postulated that water might exist at lower levels. In that case, Venus might be like the Earth in the Carboniferous Era, with seas, vegetation — even dinosaur-like monsters — an idea which SF authors were quick to adopt. Or there could be oceans of soda-water, since carbon dioxide was a gas that *had* been discovered there and is water-soluble.

The alternative, which Bonestell (like Mel Hunter, opposite) preferred, was an arid, wind-blown dust-bowl in which rocks were eroded into weird sculptures by flying particles. Rudaux portrayed it as a more mundane desert. The reality is more fantastic than any of these: a retrograde (backward) rotation period of 243 days and a 'year' of nearly 225 days, a maximum surface temperature of 485°C due to a runaway greenhouse effect, and clouds composed of sulphuric acid droplets, showering acid rain.

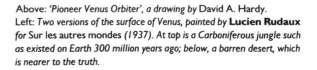

Above: 'Pioneer Venus Orbiter', a drawing by David A. Hardy.
Left: *Two versions of the surface of Venus, painted by* **Lucien Rudaux** *for* Sur les autres mondes *(1937). At top is a Carboniferous jungle such as existed on Earth 300 million years ago; below, a barren desert, which is nearer to the truth.*

Right, top: **Mel Hunter** *painted a hot, dry Venus, with its rocks eroded into weird sculptures by wind-blown dust for the book* Nine Planets *(1960, courtesy of the artist).*

Right, below: *'Sunset on Venus' by* **Helmut K. Wimmer** *(poster colours, 18 × 12 in/457 × 305 mm, courtesy of the artist). This was commissioned by Smithsonian magazine and represents the distortion of the Sun's disc by the dense atmosphere of Venus. The circular image is at the zenith and it flattens as it sets; an observer would appear to be standing inside a bowl, as the horizon curves due to 'supercritical refraction'.*

Artist Profile

HELMUT K. WIMMER

Helmut Wimmer was born in Munich, Germany, in 1925 and had early training as a sculptor and architectural model-maker. Captured by Czech partisans six days *after* the war ended, he was held by the Russians as a prisoner of war for over four years, working as a lumberjack. After release, from 1949, he restored several of Munich's fine buildings which had suffered war damage. He emigrated to the United States in 1954 (with no knowledge of English) and almost immediately began to work at the Hayden Planetarium in New York City, becoming its Art Supervisor until 1987.

He considers himself an illustrator, and his first work appeared in 1958 in a series of children's books written by Dr Franklyn M. Branley. He has since contributed to *Natural History*, the *Smithsonian*, the *Reader's Digest*, *Graphis*, the *National Geographic*, the *New York Times* and several other publications.

He works in poster colours or acrylic, and uses an airbrush or just brushwork. He developed his own technique of airbrush illustration for the famous 'Sky Shows' at the planetarium, where his paintings continue to be a main feature of the show.

Helmut says that he is now retired, but his work stands as an international language.

In 1974, when it was on its way to Mercury, Mariner 10 was the first to show that the clouds of Venus have a swirling, spiral structure when seen in ultraviolet light. In 1978 the Pioneer Venus orbiter showed these in colour (yellowish). Within them are extremely rapid lightning strokes. And as a final oddity, the clouds have their own rotation period of four days.

Artist Profile

ANDREI SOKOLOV

Born in 1931, People's Artist Andrei Sokolov graduated from the Moscow Institute of Architecture in 1955. He was inspired by the first manned spaceflight by Yuri Gagarin in 1961, and also by science fiction such as *Fahrenheit 451* by Ray Bradbury, and began to interpret both in paint.

His work has now been exhibited in the Soviet Union for over 30 years. A series of books of his work sold out almost immediately after they were published. He works mainly in acrylics and his subject matter is wide: from accurate documentation of space projects to futuristic scenes, from impressionistic and abstract subjects to fantasy.

Andrei's most popular works are probably those depicting actual space missions, such as Soyuz flights, Salyut and Mir space stations and extravehicular activities (EVAs). He often collaborates with his close friend, Cosmonaut Alexei Leonov, a skilled amateur artist, who checks details of views from spacecraft from the advantage of having been there. Their work (done together and singly) has toured the Soviet Union, Europe and the USA, and appeared in several books and on postage stamps. Other cosmonauts also take his sketches into orbit to answer his questions.

The National Air and Space Museum owns several Sokolov originals, and his work is in the joint IAAA/Soviet exhibition. He is head of the new section of the Artists' Union for 'Cosmic Art'. His work is available in the West through Space Art International, thanks to the efforts of Frederick C. Durant, III, its Conservator.

The USSR has had a great deal of success in exploring Venus, as Sokolov shows here. After three previous attempts had failed, Venera 4 made a night landing by parachute in 1967, Veneras 5 and 6 landed in 1969, and Venera 7 made the first *soft* landing in 1970. The first pictures were sent back by Venera 9 in October 1975 and showed sharp-edged rocks, which suggest that they had either formed recently (by volcanism) or were exposed by faulting.

Volcanoes there certainly are. In 1973 radar scans showed vast, shallow craters, and later radar images, backed up by both US and Soviet probes, revealed 'continents' — elevated areas on the vast, cratered plain which covers 50 per cent of the surface. Venera 8 surprised scientists by showing that the lowlands seem to be composed of a material similar to terrestrial granite, rather than the basalt expected. What appear to be impact craters (despite the dense, eroding atmosphere) are found mainly in the lowland areas, not highland as on the Moon and Mars. There are lava flows, a huge rift valley and massive shield volcanoes of the type that comprise the Hawaiian Islands, but even larger.

Two of four probes dropped by Pioneer Venus 2 fell on the night side. At a height of about 9 miles/14 km they detected a strange glow, which increased as they approached the surface. This could be caused by high-temperature chemical reactions in the hellish, sulphurous brew near the surface, or may be electrical in nature.

It would take a brave visionary to suggest a manned base on Venus, but the latest method of exploration is by balloon. A dirigible probe filled with hydrogen could float around for many weeks, relaying data via an orbiter.

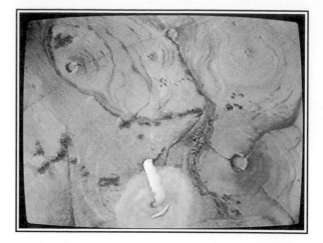

The Red Planet We have already seen that artists' visions, which depend upon the observations of astronomers and the theories of scientists, have had to change many times over the decades. Nowhere is this more so than on Mars. From having blue skies (because it has an atmosphere), uninteresting expanses of rusty desert relieved by straight, vegetation-lined canals, it went through a phase of being disappointingly Moon-like. That was in 1965 when Mariner 4 skimmed past at just under 6200 miles/10,000 km and transmitted 21 historic, black and white close-ups.

When Viking 1 transmitted its first images from Chryse Planitia in July 1976, scientists were prepared by the many reconstructions of artists to see a dark blue sky, due to the thin atmosphere. The first surprise was that the sky was so bright — comparable with Earth's. Scientists at the Jet Propulsion Laboratory (JPL) were worried by the reddish glow that bathed both sky and ground, so they adjusted their filters to give the sky a neutral grey tint. In photographic reproductions this took on a blue tone, so the first pictures released to the media showed a scene which could have been the Arizona desert. Later comparisons with colour scales and orange wiring on the lander showed that the sky was indeed orange-pink, due to suspended dust particles which scatter the Sun's light.

More by accident than prescience, perhaps, some artists got it right (above). In the 1955 George Pal film *Conquest of Space*, Bonestell's matte backgrounds showed Mars to have both volcanic and meteoritic craters, with cracks forming 'canals'. Valigursky also showed a Mars with giant crevasses.

Right: 'Automatic Rocket Surveying Mars' by British artist **Leslie Carr** (based on a drawing by R. A. Smith). This illustration from Arthur C. Clarke's 1951 book The Exploration of Space compares favourably with Bonestell's work of the period, and also looks remarkably modern, with its exposed motors, struts and wiring. At right are the tiny moons, Phobos and Deimos.

Right, below: 'Viking One' by **Mark Maxwell** (detail; original in acrylics on canvas, 24 × 30 in/610 × 762 mm, collection of Ken and Janet Shavor, TRW, Inc., Huntsville, courtesy of the artist). The 1976 Viking landers and orbiters relayed an immense amount of data about the red planet.

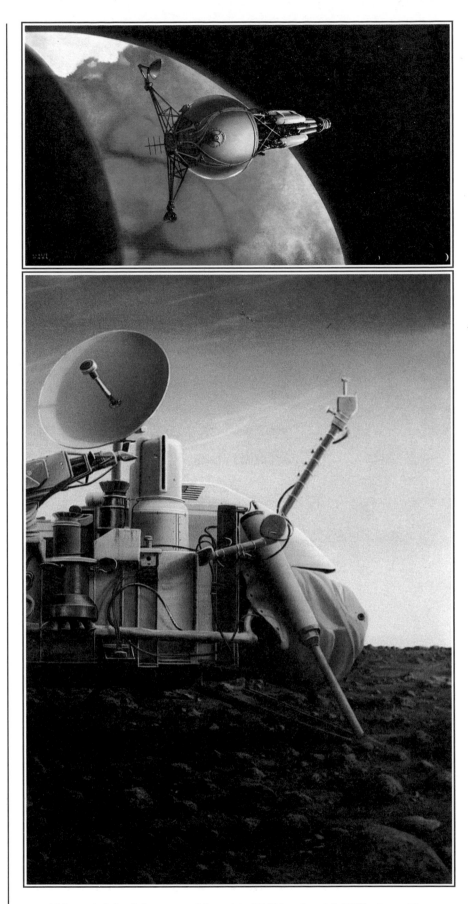

Artist Profile

KURT C. BURMANN

Kurt Carlton Burmann was born in 1956 and lives in Armada, Michigan. He is self-taught as an artist, and graduated from MIT International Space University in 1987 (the first graduating class).

He lists his influences in space art as Chesley Bonestell, Robert T. McCall, David A. Hardy and Adolph Schaller.

He first produced his own space art in 1976 and freelanced from 1978. He paints in acrylics with water-colours, using combined airbrush and dry brush techniques to achieve an effect of hyper-realism; he is both fine artist and illustrator. His major work to date is a 10 × 16-ft/3 × 5-m mural, 'Quest for the Calling', on space exploration and extraterrestrial intelligence at Detroit Science Center. He has lectured for the National Commission on Space.

In 1984 Kurt's work appeared on the March and June covers of Space World, a magazine published by the National Space Society, and in Sky and Telescope (February 1986). It is also included in the Asimov 'Library of the Universe' series, among other publications. He has taken part in many exhibitions, including 'Visions of Space' at Detroit Science Center (1985), 'The Case for Mars' conference (Planetary Society, 1986), 'Spacefair 87' conference (in collaboration with Kim P. Poor) at the Institute of Technology, Boston, and the IAAA exhibition 'Other Worlds'. His solo exhibition, 'Celestial Voyage', was held at Denver Museum of Natural History during 1988–89. He says, 'Until everyone can travel the universe, the space artist has to be the eye of all who still have their feet rooted on this planet.'

Although it had the same title as his 1949 book with Willy Ley, *Conquest of Space* had much more in common with the later *Exploration of Mars* (1956). The terrain of Mars, though (in which Bonestell had no hand), was inaccurate according to the science of the day, even if some of the special effects were an improvement on previous Pal films. But Bonestell did also paint a fault valley full of fog for the later book — a forerunner of Pat Rawlings's dramatic scene on pages 94–5.

© Kurt C. Burmann '86

A New Frontier Mars has proved a fascinating world and is now probably the subject of more activity among space artists than any other. This is at least partly due to the activity of the Planetary Society (which is US-based but international) and its founder, Dr Carl Sagan. For some years they have been vigorously promoting the scientific exploration of Mars and encouraging collaboration between the USA and the USSR to that end. A 'Mars Declaration' was issued in 1988 and signed by hundreds of prominent scientists, astronomers and others, asking the major governments of this world to support such peaceful cooperation in space. Its 'Mars '94 Project' proposes a joint US, Soviet and French balloon probe.

As Carl Sagan has pointed out, the US has not launched a *single* mission to the Moon or planets since 1978. He sees the goal of Mars as a new focus for the US civilian space programme, bringing together NASA's various constituencies. Just as in the case of the *Collier's* assault on the public in the 1950s, artists are in the front line — and this time there are many more of them. The Planetary Society is working hand in glove with the International Association for the Astronomical Arts, to which most of the artists in this

Above: 'Dread of War' by **Kurt C. Burmann** (1986, acrylics, courtesy of the artist). When Asaph Hall discovered the moons of Mars in 1877, he named them Phobos and Deimos ('fear' and 'dread') after the handmaidens of Mars, the god of war. Thanks to Viking and other probes, we now believe them to be captured asteroids; they consist of very dark, carbonaceous material. Here we see Deimos, 14,000 miles/23,000 km from Mars and an irregular 9 × 7 miles/15 × 12 km in diameter.
Right: Two typically realistic views of Mars by **Ludek Pesek** (both oils, 24 × 35 ½ in/610 × 900 mm, courtesy of the artist). Top, the icy polar region. Much of the 'ice' is, in fact, carbon dioxide 'dry ice'. Bottom, part of the incredible canyon system Valles Marineris.

Kazuaki Iwasaki 1057

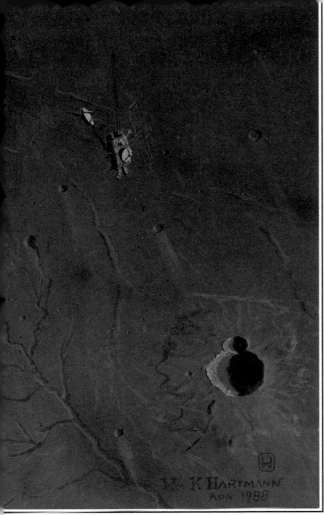

Above: Aerial view of Mars by **William K. Hartmann** (acrylics, courtesy of the artist). We look down, from a higher orbit, on a probe as it scans the giant volcanoes.

Left: 'Twin Peaks: Ceraunius and Uranius' by **Kazuaki Iwasaki** (water-colour on smooth paper, 17 1/4 × 13 3/4 in/438 × 350 mm; courtesy of the artist) gives a more oblique view of two volcanic cones.

Right: In 'Phobos Encounter' (acrylics on canvas board, 15 × 18 in/ 380 × 458 mm, courtesy of the artist) **Arthur Gilbert** painted a preview of the planned experiment for the Soviet Phobos 2 probe to fire a laser beam from within 160 ft/50 m to analyse the gases. Sadly, the probe went out of control.

Artist Profile

ARTHUR GILBERT

Although born in 1936, Arthur Gilbert is 'one of the newer fellers' in space art. He lives in Alfreton, Derbyshire, and is self-taught as an artist.

Arthur's interest in space and its art goes back to boyhood, when he read the *Eagle* comic with its adventures of 'Dan Dare, Pilot of the Future'. He was influenced by US comics and science-fiction magazines, then later by Bonestell's work in *Conquest of Space* and Hardy's in *Challenge of the Stars*, and finally TV coverage of the Apollo missions.

He began to paint space subjects in the mid-1970s and was first published in *Space World* magazine in 1988. He thinks of himself as an artist first, illustrator second — perhaps 70:30. His major work to date is 'Erosion on Io'; the original, a large oil-painting, was published in *Space World*. He uses oils, or acrylics for faster drying time, and sketches in pencil or inks.

An exhibition of his work was held at the Ilkeston Astronomy Club in the summer of 1989. His future intentions are possibly to turn towards impressionism or surrealism in an attempt to capture the theme of creation, or mankind's view of a creator, and perhaps to combine this with poetry to the same end. He also aims to boost public awareness of astronomy through local exhibitions.

book belong, and has subsidized exhibitions and meetings between Western and Soviet artists (more about that in the final section).

Sagan opposes the establishment of a base on the Moon before going to Mars. He sees a joint US/Soviet programme as proceeding via, first, rover, balloon and sample return missions, and points out that both scientifically and in terms of public interest, Mars is more interesting than the Moon. Commitment to a lunar base, he says, could delay a Mars mission by decades.

To the argument that a manned mission to Mars would be too expensive, he replies that such a mission is estimated to cost as much as a single major strategic weapons system. One might think that the public would have little difficulty in choosing which would be of greater benefit, especially given the spirit in which such an enterprise would be undertaken.

The terrain of Mars is certainly dramatic and inspiring for artists, as well as being of great scientific and geological interest. The incredible system of interlinked chasms and gorges which form the Valles Marineris stretches nearly a third of the way around the planet; Colorado's Grand Canyon would be lost inside it. There are strange, sinuous channels which look remarkably like dried-up river-beds, and icy polar regions where great sedimentary deposits can be found. But above all, quite literally, are the giant volcanoes.

In 1879 the Director of Milan Observatory, Giovanni Schiaparelli (who was the first astronomer to observe what he called *canali* (channels) crossing the Martian deserts, sparking off the whole mystery of canals and little green men that pervaded astronomy and science fiction for so long) noticed a brilliant white spot about 20 degrees north of the equator. He christened it Nix Olympia (Snows of Olympus, home of the Greek gods), because he took it to *be* snow, even though it appeared only in summer.

It is actually the cone of probably the largest volcano in the Solar System, since named Olympus Mons by the IAU, and stands some 15 miles/25 km high, while its base extends for over 370 miles/600 km. The bright spot observed by Schiaparelli may have been caused by an isolated condensation cloud as air rises and cools over the vast cone. In the same area, known as the Tharsis region, are three other large extinct volcanoes, while another groups occurs in the Elysium region.

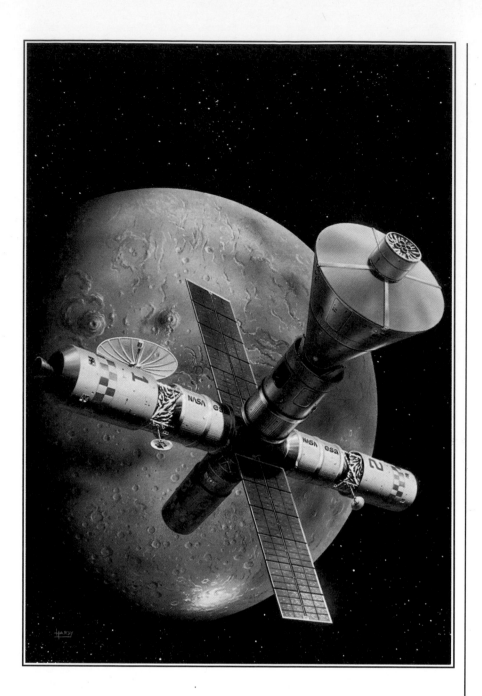

Left: 'Mars in 1995!' by **David A. Hardy** (gouache, 17 × 12 in/430 × 305 mm, collection of Bob Parkinson). In 1981 Dr Robert C. Parkinson of the BIS undertook a design study on a 'minimal' manned mission, which could reach Mars in 1995, using existing NASA hardware, with the ESA Spacelab as crew quarters. This is one of three paintings illustrating the mission, used in Analog (June 1981) and later in Spaceflight and other BIS publications. The three ships have docked in a cruciform formation, solar panels extended, and the conical lander is being separated.

(Page 86–7) 'Elysium 1' by **Larry Ortiz** (acrylics, 15 × 20 in/380 × 508 mm, courtesy of the artist) is one of a projected series of six paintings of Mars, based on Viking orbiter photographs. Each is painted from the same point on the surface and at 2.00 p.m. local time.

Artist Profile

DOUGLAS CHAFFEE

Doug Chaffee was born in 1936 and gained a degree in art education, but is largely self-taught in illustration. He lives in Taylors, South Carolina.

His interest in space was sparked, around 1945, by Skyman comics and Flash Gordon, then by films of the 1950s and science-fiction illustrators Frank Kelly Freas and Ed Emshwiller. He first produced his own space art in 1951, and from 1966 to 1967 worked for the IBM Corporation, *National Geographic, US News, Newsweek* and *Galaxy* magazines. He contributed to the National Geographic Society's highly-illustrated *Our Universe* (1980), along with such artists as Davis Meltzer, Pesek, Miller, Hartmann, Wimmer and SF artists Michael Whelan and Vincent di Fate.

Doug uses acrylics, inks and pencils to present as realistic and detailed a view as possible of a hypothetical scene. He exhibited in the 1960s at the National Association of Industrial Artists, Washington, DC, from 1973 to 1980 at the Smithsonian Institution, and in 1982 at the Nature Museum and Planetarium, Charlotte, North Carolina.

He estimates that the types of art he currently produces could be divided thus: SF and fantasy, 20 per cent; military, 10 per cent; astronomical, 5 per cent; biblical, 60 per cent; agency and general, 5 per cent. His aim is 'to produce the SF and space art that will hang in the homes of the coming generation of spacefarers', and he is currently involved in rendering a corporation's private space shuttle endeavour.

Artists on Mars Some artists are particularly drawn towards Mars. MariLynn Flynn (although due to the constraints of space — no pun intended — none of her paintings of Mars appear here) has done a study of 'Martian analogues' — terrestrial counterparts of Martian features, such as the shield volcanoes which are found in Hawaii and Iceland. Perhaps the best-known painter of Mars is Ludek Pesek, who now lives in Switzerland and has illustrated articles for *National Geographic* magazine and many books. Born in 1919, he was in his forties before he painted astronomical subjects professionally. His first two books, *The Moon and Planets* (1963) and *Our Planet Earth* (1967) are now collectors' items.

For the February 1973 issue of *National Geographic*, Pesek painted a number of Martian scenes, one of which was issued as a full-size print. This depicted a dust storm, a favourite subject of the artist since. The scientific information at that time came from the Mariner 9 spacecraft.

An admitted romantic, Pesek paints in oils or acrylics in a looser and more impressionistic style than many other space artists, although he sometimes uses an airbrush (sparingly) for skies and clouds. But the most attractive feature of Pesek's work is its credibility, as the two works on page 83 show. His scenes have what might be called 'personality'.

Another artist who is well known for his scenes on Mars, as well as the Moon, but is more interested in the presence of Man there, is Robert McCall. Using acrylics, he paints in a variety of styles, from very loose and sketchy to quite detailed. Anyone who has visited the National Air and Space Museum in Washington, DC, cannot have missed his work, as a vast mural symbolizing the conquest of the Moon occupies an entire wall near the main entrance. He began as an aviation artist, and among the books containing his work are *Our World in Space* with Isaac Asimov (1974) and *Vision of the Future* with text by Ben Bova (1982), two volumes that should be in every collection of space art.

More recently, McCall contributed a cover and illustrations for *Pioneering the Space Frontier* (1986), the Report of the National Commission on Space. Two of these appear here on page 93 and show Mars settlements of the twenty-first century. (Another very intriguing illustration in that report contrasts a modern view of a space station and Shuttle with Bonestell's 1950s' version.) He has also designed postage stamps and astronauts' spacesuit patches, and in 1988 was inducted into the Society of Illustrators' Hall of Fame, an honour which places him in the company of N.C. Wyeth and Norman Rockwell (who has also painted space subjects), among others.

Perhaps the most outstanding aspect of McCall's work, apart from its technical and artistic excellence, is its optimism. His future, although highly technological, always appears bright and attractive to live in, and Mars looks as inviting a place for our descendants to live as Earth, if not more so.

The other artists in these pages have painted various aspects of Mars, both its landscapes and the effects of Man's arrival there. Although based on the same information, it is interesting to compare how the various interpretations differ in treatment and technique. Paul Hudson (above) has perhaps the most photographic style of all, and his work is extremely detailed and painstaking; yet any student of the genre will identify his work, and most of the others', almost immediately. Bonestell's work was often called

'Mars Rover' by **Paul Hudson** *(acrylics, © Thomasson-Grant, Inc., courtesy of the artist) has a pressurized cabin for three crew members, and water and electricity drawn from fuel cells. Samples can be gathered using the robot arms without the astronauts leaving the vehicle, but, if necessary, they can put on suits, as here, to investigate an area more closely.*

photographic, but today, as Ron Miller has pointed out, it often seems to have a neat, orderly and almost park-like appearance. Many contemporary artists make a deliberate effort to overcome this, as he does, by introducing random factors when painting, and by using photographic references of Earth landscapes, rocks and so on as a starting point.

Miller is another artist who has often concentrated on Mars. His article, 'Space Art' in the August 1988 issue of the BIS journal *Spaceflight* makes

Artist Profile

PAUL HUDSON

Paul Hudson was born in 1960 and spent two terms at the Art Center in Pasadena, California. He lives in North Bend, Washington State.

Paul was nine when Apollo 11 landed on the Moon, and was captivated by the drama, tension and magic of space travel as he grew up. He says that the first thing he drew was a rocket. His first published work, for the Jet Propulsion Laboratory (JPL), was a series of paintings depicting future spacecraft. He considers himself a fine artist (with which no one would disagree).

His work has appeared in *The Solar System* (part of Time-Life's 'Planet Earth' series, 1985), *National Geographic, Discover, Newton, Aviation Week* and NASA publications. He says he has yet to create his major work.

In 1988 Paul and former Boeing associate Brand Norman Griffin started 'Spaceworks', whereby Brand provides engineering concepts and Paul paints the hardware in space. The first results appeared in the large-format 1989 *Spaceworks Calendar*. He also produces work for the Orbital Sciences Corporation in Fairfax, Virginia.

Paul says that when not producing space art he paints his beautiful wife, Colette, whom he married in 1988.

Artist Profile

LARRY ORTIZ

Larry Ortiz was born in 1948 and, after an extensive liberal arts education in the California education system in the 1970s, obtained an Associate in Arts degree. He lives in San Diego.

In addition to doing astronomical art, he is a video and film production designer. His influences, he says, were many: from Bonestell and McCall in the space art field to Byron Haskin, George Pal, Stanley Kubrick, Ridley Scott and Douglas Trumbull in the world of imaginative film production, and past masters such as Albrecht Dürer, the Van Eycks, Bosch, the Bruegels and Walt Disney.

Larry's first piece of actual space art was executed in 1977, entitled 'Martian Anomaly'. In late 1982 he produced two matte paintings, one of Mercury (page 75) and one of Mars, for the Fleet Space Theater, San Diego. Since then his work has appeared in such magazines as *Space World* and *Planetary Report*, NASA illustrated reports, *Industrialization of the Solar System* (1984), and several other publications.

A short 35mm film made in 1982, concerning the fate of two hapless astronauts on Mars and featuring a cameo by SF author Greg Bear, won first place at the School of Visual Arts in New York City. His major work to date, to which his wife, Laurie, contributed charts and graphs, was 'Advanced Propulsion Systems for LEO—LLO Transit' (Low Earth Orbit — Low Lunar Orbit). He is also proud of the 'Elysium' series of paintings, one of which is reproduced on pages 86–7. He paints in acrylics, from dark to light, using dry brush techniques and some airbrush. His work has appeared in many exhibitions, and he also does SF cover art.

Above and right: *Two paintings by* **Robert T. McCall** *of a Mars Outpost, used to illustrate* Pioneering the Space Frontier *(1986, top, 24 × 34 in/610 × 864 mm; bottom, 48 × 72 in/1220 × 1830 mm, both acrylics, © Bantam Press, courtesy of the artist). Both depict a twenty-first-century Mars settlement with living quarters, and spaceports where landers arrive and depart.*

Left: *Three paintings from* **Carter Emmart's** *'The Case for Mars' series, using existing technology (1986, all magic marker on paper, 20 × 18 in/508 × 457 mm, courtesy of the artist). Produced for a JPL video.*
Top: *The base is set up at a safe distance from the landers' future blast-off point. The cargo vehicles are connected nose to tail for use as a dwelling.*
Centre: *Inflatable greenhouses are added to supply food and, with the crew, form a partially closed biological system.*
Bottom: *Drag lines are used to scoop soil and cover the habitat for protection against solar radiation, which the thin Martian atmosphere and weak magnetic field do not provide.*

interesting reading, and he is the author of the first book devoted to the work of space artists: *Space Art* (1978). He is also co-author and co-illustrator of *The Grand Tour* (1981), *Out of the Cradle* (1984) and *Cycles of Fire* (1987). (Ron's brother, Tom Miller, also contributed artwork to the last title.)

Ron Miller's friend and collaborator Bill Hartmann is one of the few space artists to start out as a professional astronomer and scientist and later turn to art, rather than the reverse. An adviser to NASA and senior scientist

'First Light' (*Exploration of the Noctis Labyrinthus canyon system on Mars*) by **Pat Rawlings** (*acrylics, 18 × 36 in/457 × 915 mm, Eagle Engineering artwork for NASA Office of Exploration, courtesy of the artist). To produce this artwork a relief map based on Viking orbiter data was built from paper towels and plaster of Paris. Once sculpted, it was lit by a slide projector representing the Sun. Photographs were taken through a wide-angle lens, then fitted together like a mosaic to form a panorama about 90 degrees wide. The early morning fog, formed when the rising Sun vaporizes ices on east-facing slopes, was photographed in this area by Viking orbiter. (Note the frost in the shadows.)*

at the Planetary Science Institute with a particular interest in planetary geology, he has also written his own books, such as *Astronomy: The Cosmic Journey* (1978). He is particularly concerned by the fact that many scientists seem unable to visualize the phenomena which they see only as masses of data or as graphs on a VDU, and is therefore a powerful advocate of the realistic school of space art.

Left: 'Oasis' by **Mark Dowman** (1985, acrylics, 27 × 18 in/686 × 457 mm, Eagle Engineering/NASA). Phobos space station supports surface activities, propellant storage depot, docking and hangar facilities.

Pamela Lee (below) has a particular interest in the human aspects of space exploration, as several of her beautiful renderings in this book reveal. But she can as easily turn her hand to the technological side, as do Mark Dowman and Paul DiMare here. They see operations in Mars–orbit and at its tiny moon Phobos (see also page 82) as an essential stage in maintaining surface activities on the red planet.

Artist Profile

CARTER EMMART

Born in 1961, Carter Emmart gained a BS in geophysics from the University of Colorado in 1984, and he was the original organizer of the university's Space Interest Group, which sponsored the 'Case for Mars' conference series. He lives in Demarest, New Jersey.

He has very early memories of a fascination with astronomy, scale and infinity, and grew up with an artistic family legacy. At the age of 15 he won a contest organized by the Hayden Planetarium, and he was first published at the age of 18. Although both a fine artist and illustrator, he separates the two, but says that his illustration strives to be the clearest representation of functionality, while also being inspirational.

Carter has contributed to a video production, *Together to Mars*, and to the Jet Propulsion Laboratory (JPL) video *Mars — the Next Step*, among others, and the book *Race to Mars* (1988), while Random House has a book of his work in production.

Exhibitions of his work include the Propulsion Conference at MIT and JPL (1988), Hayden Planetarium (October 1988–June 1989), and several more. He also produces computer graphics, sculptures and models.

Cosmic Debris We have been moving gradually further from the Sun in our artistic tour of the Solar System. Beyond Mars is a very wide gap before we reach Jupiter, but this gap contains many small bodies held roughly together in what are called the Asteroid Belts. Contrary to the impression given by films such as *The Empire Strikes Back*, such belts are not closely-packed masses of hurtling rocks; it would probably be rare to see one asteroid from another, except as a moving 'star'.

The largest of them, Ceres, is little more than 620 miles/1000 km in diameter, and most are much smaller. Their interest to space artists is usually their potential in supplying valuable minerals for the Earth or future space colonies, or as 'asteroid arks' (page 127) for long interstellar voyages. Or, as in Don Davis's rather worrying painting (opposite), in the effect that even quite a small-sized errant asteroid would have if its orbit intersected that of Earth at the wrong moment.... Indeed, this may have happened some 65 million years ago, creating a sort of 'non-nuclear winter' that resulted in the extinction of the dinosaurs (page 100).

Another Solar System vagrant is the comet. As with an eclipse, it is no surprise that a great comet's nebulous tail, appearing night after night, used to provoke reactions of alarm or worship. Thanks to the probes to Halley's Comet in 1986, we now know much more. Comets are *very* dirty snowballs, and there is a spherical cloud of them at the periphery of the Solar System.

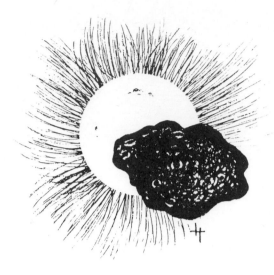

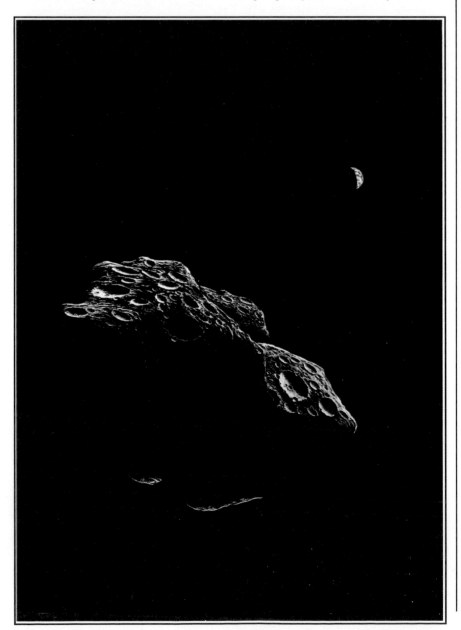

Above: 'Asteroid Icarus Near the Sun', a drawing by David A. Hardy.
Left: 'Asteroid' by **Hans Martens** (gouache, 12 × 16½ in/300 × 420 mm, courtesy of the artist). Left over from the Solar System's formation, asteroids are the remaining bodies in space which could still make craters on the Earth — at any time. Those which cross Earth's orbit, as here, are called Apollo asteroids.
Right: 'Orbital View of Impact' by **Don Davis** (acrylics, courtesy of the artist). The awesome sight of a large asteroid entering Earth's atmosphere — with devastating results. Even if it landed in an ocean, massive tidal waves (tsunamis) and atmospheric blast effects would create havoc.

(Page 97) Above: 'Manned Mission to Mars' by **Paul DiMare** (gouache, 16 × 24 in/406 × 610 mm, courtesy of the artist). Two astronauts deploy a communications satellite (one of three for global coverage). Lander in distance.
Below: 'Together to Mars' by **Pamela Lee** — a cosmonaut and astronaut survey the red planet together from low Mars orbit.

Left, top: 'Portent of Doom' by **Julian Baum** (photograph using model and painted background, courtesy of the artist). Comets have long been regarded as harbingers of doom and disaster, and it seems that this was never more true than when one appeared in the skies of Earth 65 million years ago. For it may have been the nucleus of a large comet that struck the Earth, creating a massive dust cloud that blotted out the Sun for years, that was responsible for the extinction of many species.

Left, below: 'Moment of Extinction' by **David A. Hardy** (gouache, 18 × 15 in/458 × 380 mm, collection of Donald R. Brady, Jr). Tyrannosaurus rex snarls defiance as a huge fireball streaks through the upper atmosphere; already shockwaves whip vegetation and cause the ground to shake. Soon, only his fossilized bones will remain — if anything.

Artist Profile

JULIAN BAUM

Julian Baum was born in 1960 and gained a City and Guilds certificate in general photography. He lives in Boughton, near Chester, and is one of three English members of the IAAA.

His father, Richard Baum, is an amateur astronomer and writer, and a prominent member of the British Astronomical Society, so Julian was exposed to astronomy from early childhood. At the age of five his imagination was fired by a book entitled You Will Go to the Moon (illustrated by Robert Patterson, 1959); later on Hardy's Challenge of the Stars brought his enthusiasm into focus. Seeing the opening sequence of Star Wars finally proved the catalyst that spurred him into action.

Julian's technique is unusual among modern space artists, although Nasmyth and Scriven Bolton must have used similar, if primitive, means to obtain their results. He is an expert photographer and combines model-building and colour photography with painted backgrounds by sophisticated methods. (Only Brian Sullivan in the USA does anything similar, although British photographer Michael Freeman has produced space subjects.) Julian's first experiments were made when he was 16, in 1976.

His work has appeared in Asimov's 'Library of the Universe' series and the British Interplanetary Society's journal, Spaceflight, and he produces maps and projections of the Earth for London's Science Photo Library. He prepared effects slides and organized programmes for Liverpool Planetarium in 1980–81, and has plans for exhibitions in the future. He has a great interest in 'alternative futures': 'What happens now determines whether the future will be an overindustrialized and overcrowded nightmare, a barren, war-blasted planet with a dying people, a space-going society, or — what?'

Artist Profile

THOMAS L. HUNT

Tom Hunt was born in 1951 and gained a BA in visual communications from the University of Wisconsin, Milwaukee, in 1976. He lives in Racine, Wisconsin.

Following a long interest in astronomy, he started working for *Astronomy* magazine in 1979 as Art Director. Thanks to its founder, the late Stephen A. Walther, this magazine has a long tradition of using astronomical art, which was particularly strong in the 1970s, and for many people it introduced the work of Mark Paternostro and Adolf Schaller. (The work of some of its other 'regular' artists, such as Victor Costanzo, John Clark, Steve R. Dodd and David Egge, is rarely seen nowadays; presumably they have moved into other fields.) Tom's work there and in other Kalmbach publications is seen by 300,000 people worldwide every month.

His work also appears in the Time-Life series on the Universe, the German magazine *Stern*, and other books and posters. His airbrush painting of Halley's Comet (right) was used on the book, *Comet Halley*, which sold over 100,000 copies in several languages. It also appeared in *Astronomy* magazine and was used as a promotional poster for the State of Michigan. The medium used was gouache. Another example of Tom's work (page 162) shows what people were doing between appearances of Halley's Comet and prompted more mail to the magazine than any other illustration.

Tom also paints other subjects, including figures and abstracts, using alkyds, oils, gouache (all with airbrush), pen and ink, pastels, and 3-D work. His goal is to 'turn people on to this fascinating subject'.

Right, top: 'Comet Halley' by **Thomas L. Hunt** *(acrylics/airbrush, 30 × 24 in/762 × 610 mm, © Astronomy, Kalmbach Publishing) depicts Halley's Comet at its finest, its semi-transparent tail of gas and dust flying. (A comet's tail is not always 'behind' it; being pushed by the pressure of solar radiation, the tail can travel first as the comet retreats from the Sun.)*
Right, below: 'Halley's Comet Nucleus' by **Jean-Michel Joly** *(1984, gouache, 27½ × 39¼ in/700 × 1000 mm, courtesy of the artist). Painted before the encounter of Giotto and other probes with Halley, this painting predicts craters and jets of gas rising from the solid, 'dirty snowball' nucleus of the comet.*

(Page 102) Left, top: 'Perturbed Body of Solar Debris Exiting the Oort Cloud, by **Mark Paternostro** *(acrylics, courtesy of the artist). In 1950 Dutch astronomer Jan Oort suggested that a vast spherical cloud of perhaps 100 billion comets surrounds the Solar System. Occasionally the orbit of one is disturbed, and it heads sunward.*
Below: 'Cometary Eruption' by **Kurt C. Burmann** *(acrylics, 14 × 26 in/355 × 660 mm, courtesy of the artist). A team of explorers is greeted by a geyser. In the low gravity, matter, once ejected, may never return.*

Artist Profile

JON LOMBERG

Born in 1948, Jon Lomberg has a BA in English literature. Although he lived until recently in Canada, he now resides in Hawaii.

He has been interested in space since the age of four, art since 17, and space art since 22. His main artistic influences were Dali, Escher and Steranko — but not Bonestell; other major influences were Sagan, Shklovskii, Heinlein, Clarke and Stapledon. He first produced his own space art in 1970, and was first published in Carl Sagan's *The Cosmic Connection* (1973). Subsequent work for Sagan includes the books *Broca's Brain* (1979), *Cosmos* (1980), *Contact* (1985) and *Comet* (1985). He has also produced SF covers, art for astronomy books and NASA.

Jon was Chief Artist on Sagan's TV series *Cosmos*, and Art Director for three PBS *Nova* shows. One of his major projects was as Designer for the Voyager 'Interstellar Record', and he has done nuclear winter animations and illustrations for network TV. His favourite work includes his 'Cosmic Metaphor' and 'SETI' paintings. He has produced murals, 3-D galaxies and globes for the Ontario Science Center, the McLaughlin Planetarium of Royal Ontario Museum and the Arizona Sonora Desert Museum.

His work has appeared in the Sputnik Anniversary show in Moscow (1987), 'Art of the Cosmos' at Berkeley Hall of Science (1987), and he had one-man shows at NASA Biosciences Center, Philadelphia (1985) and Saxe Gallery, Toronto (1980). Other art deals with biology, particle physics and the oceans. Owners of his artwork include Carl Sagan, Frank Drake and many SETI scientists.

Right: *'Comet Trees'* by **Jon Lomberg** (acrylics, 17 × 22 in/432 × 560 mm, Collection of Contemporary Art, Pushkin Museum, Moscow). In 1972 Freeman Dyson suggested that 'trees' could be bred to grow to immense heights on comets where the necessary nutrients exist.

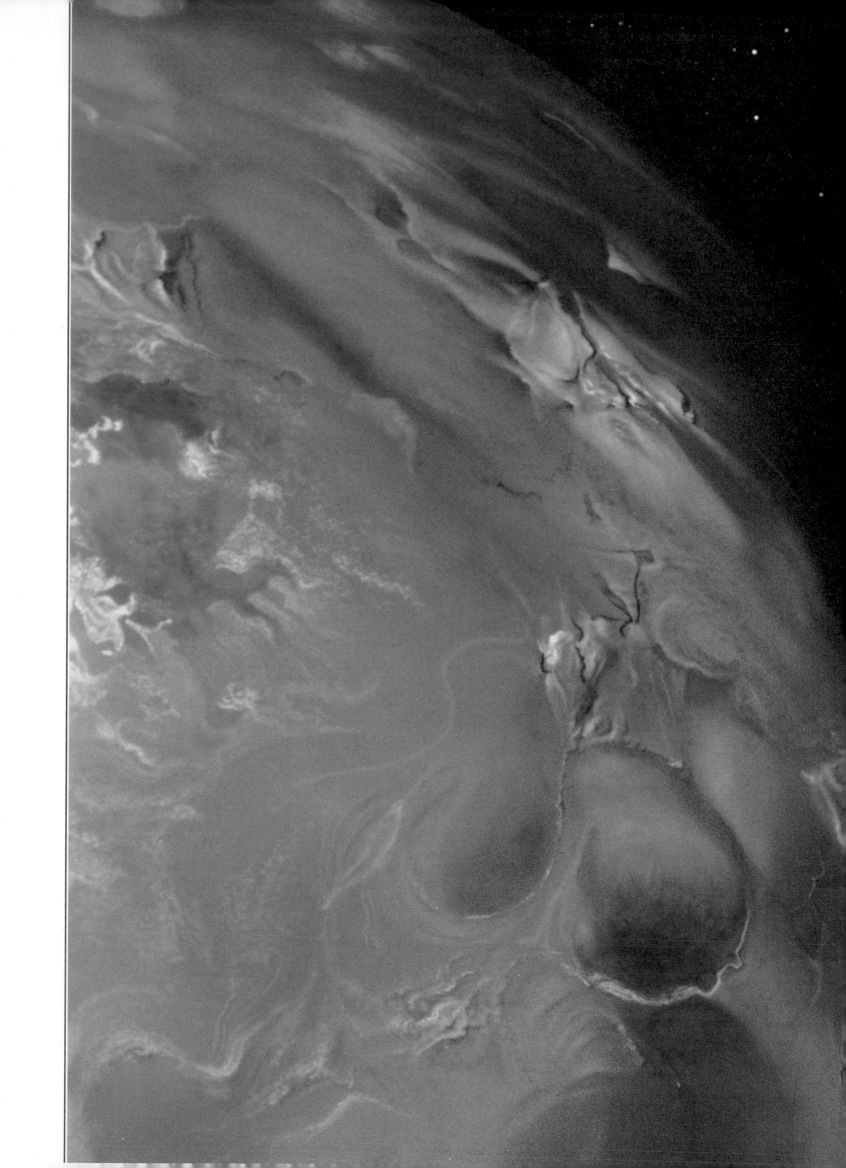

Kazuaki Iwasaki   NO 1047

The Gas Giants Beyond the asteroids we reach the region of the giant planets, of which Jupiter is king. Had the building materials of the original nebula not run out when they did, Jupiter might have grown massive enough to 'ignite' and become a star, and the present Solar System would not exist. It is nearly 90,000 miles/143,000 km in diameter, and its famous Great Red Spot could easily swallow the Earth.

We have already seen several examples of eclipses of the Sun by the Moon or the Earth. It is a remarkable astronomical coincidence that, from the Earth, the Moon covers the Sun almost exactly. Quite a different situation exists in the scene by Frank Kelly Freas (below). The Sun would be a bright, tiny disc totally dwarfed by the bulk of Jupiter, whose dense atmosphere would form a ring of light. Freas has a special place in the fields of both science-fiction and space art because he designed the posters promoting NASA's Apollo project (page 56), and has been nominated for no less than 17 Hugo Awards (SF's Oscar), winning nine. Here he postulates crystals of ilmenite on Jupiter's moon Ganymede.

Left, below: 'Eclipse from Ganymede' by **Frank Kelly Freas** (1979, acrylics, 20 × 15 in/508 × 380 mm, for The Art of Science Fiction (1979, courtesy of the artist). Here Kelly Freas speculated on the possibility of crystals of ilmenite (a natural ore of titanium, FeTiO$_3$) on one of Jupiter's large moons.

(Pages 104–5) 'Galileo Probe at Io' by **Kazuaki Iwasaki** (watercolours on smooth paper, 17 × 11¼ in/426 × 285 mm, courtesy of the artist). The first close-up pictures of Io were taken by Voyager I on 5 March 1979, and scientists were excited by active volcanoes and lava flows. This is an accurate reconstruction of the scene.

(Pages 108–9) 'Rough Weather' by **Bob Eggleton** (acrylics, 12 × 28 in/305 × 711 mm, courtesy of the artist). A ship from Earth, with solar panels and rotating living quarters, in very close proximity to Jupiter's Great Red Spot — the largest hurricane in the Solar System. Because of the tremendous radiation in this area, humans would probably never get this close; but, as in Clarke's short story 'Jupiter Five', this ship is shielded by the bulk of the oddly-shaped moon Amalthea.

(Pages 110–11) Left, top: 'Red Spot' by **Kazuaki Iwasaki** (16¾ × 12 in/427 × 304 mm).
Left, below: 'Jupiter Cloudscape' by **Adolf Schaller** (from a 7½ × 10-ft/2286 × 3048-mm mural).
Above: 'Inside a Gas Giant' by **Don Davis** shows the 'roots' of atmospheric spots.
(All paintings courtesy of the artists)

Artist Profile

RON MILLER

Ron Miller was born in 1947 and has a BA degree in illustration from Columbus College of Art and Design, Columbus, Ohio. He lives in Fredericksburg, Virginia.

He produced his first serious space art in 1973, but had been interested in space from childhood; his chief influences were Chesley Bonestell and Ludek Pesek. Ron's artwork was first published professionally in the *Smithsonian*, and has since appeared in dozens (if not hundreds) of publications. He says that he is an illustrator, but dislikes the distinction between illustration and fine art. As noted on page 94, he co-authored and illustrated *The Grand Tour*, *Out of the Cradle* and *Cycles of Fire*, of which he considers the last to be his major work to date.

He also wrote and compiled *Space Art*, and collaborated with Frederick C. Durant, III on *Worlds Beyond: The Art of Chesley Bonestell*, which is recommended to all wishing to know more about Bonestell, including his film and non-astronomical art work. He works in acrylics on illustration board, usually Strathmore, and uses an Iwata airbrush in moderation. He has worked for the Albert Einstein Spacearium and has exhibited in the 'Cosmos Forum'; his art is owned by Bill Hartmann, but he rarely knows who owns his work, as it is sold via shows such as those at SF conventions. His wife, Judith, is Treasurer of the IAAA.

Ron Miller sees space artists as fulfilling the function that several of America's Hudson River School of painters did at the end of the nineteenth century. Writing in the BIS journal *Spaceflight* (August 1988), he says, 'Words were one thing, but romantic images of the West's fantastic landscapes made them both real and unforgettable. I hope that I can do the same for our neighbours in space.'

Right, above: 'Jupiter from Europa' by **Bob Eggleton** (acrylics, 10 × 23 in/254 × 584 mm, courtesy of the artist), a view from an ice ravine. Also visible are the moon Io and a robot probe descending to gather and analyse ice samples. (See also pages 108–9.)

Right, below: 'Landing on Europa' by **Ron Miller** (1984, acrylics, from Out of the Cradle, courtesy of the artist). The first landing on the flat, groove-streaked surface of Europa, from which Jupiter looks 24 times as big as our Moon does to us.

Jupiter, like its icy companions Saturn, Uranus and Neptune, has no solid surface as such; there may be a metal-and-rock core radiating at some 30,000°C, but the temperature at the top of the cloud-deck is *minus* 143°C. A view of Jupiter through a small telescope shows a yellowish, flattened disc with greyish bands, and the four major or 'Galilean' satellites can often be seen as points of light. The images sent back by the Voyager I and II probes in 1979 (yes, as long ago as that) were much more exciting. Its great weather

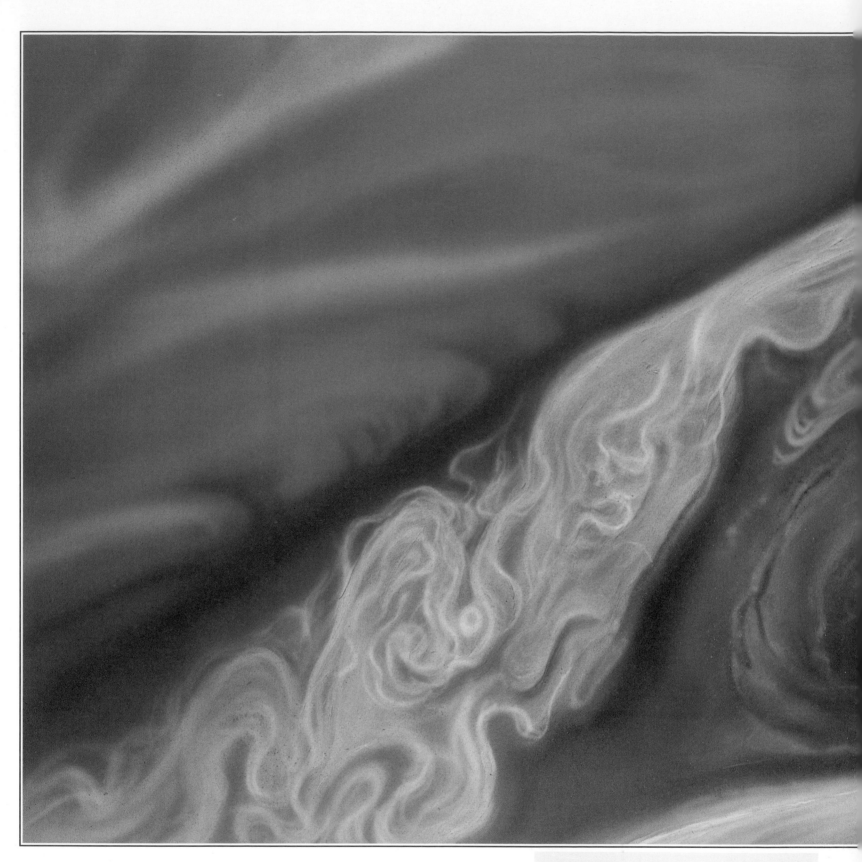

systems, hurricanes, spots and whorls appeared in magazines and books in full Technicolor — almost with stereophonic sound!

But it is true to say that this is not the view that would be obtained by an observer. Most artists tend to follow those Voyager colours, partly because the public, having accepted them as scientific evidence, expect it. Their images can also be seen as the equivalent of Earthly photographs which have been enhanced (as they often are) by the use of filters to cut haze, darken pale blue skies, or the like. And, as Bob Eggleton says in explanation of his painting on page 107, Voyager's cameras did negate the ice crystals in Jupiter's upper atmosphere, so he used the more authentic pastel tones that

Artist Profile

BOB EGGLETON

Born in 1960, Bob Eggleton studied art at Rhode Island College. He lives in Providence, Rhode Island.

His influences were Bonestell and McCall, plus Albert Beirstadt, Fredrick Church and John Constable. He produced his first space art in 1981 and was first published by Baen Books. He thinks of himself as 60 per cent illustrator, 40 per cent fine artist. He has contributed to *The Planets* (1985) and *The Universe* (1987), and at the time of writing is illustrating

the naked (not unprotected) eye would see from the icy moon Europa. Adolf Schaller's cloudscape was adapted from a 6 × 8-ft/2.3 × 3-m mural.

Japan's leading astronomical artist, Kazuaki Iwasaki, had the same intentions when he painted the delicate colours of Io during Voyager's fly-by, on pages 104–5. The first 'photographs' of Io were described as 'looking like a giant pizza', with vivid reds, oranges and yellows, but it must be remembered that pictures returned by space probes are *not* photographs taken in the normal sense, on film. They are electronic images transmitted as digital data — a series of 1s and 0s — after being collected by the hurtling spacecraft's television lenses, and are built up, pixel by pixel, on a screen after

Artist Profile

ADOLF SCHALLER

Adolf Schaller was born in 1956 and after high school studied physics and astronomy with the aid of colleagues rather than at college. He is self-taught as an artist, and his fine art print and multi-media production company, Dreamtime Productions, is run from Wheeling, Illinois.

He became interested in science at the age of six, and soon realized that both art *and* science are necessary to provide a meaningful framework in understanding nature and our relationship to it. His first nationally published work appeared on the cover of the December 1974 issue of *Astronomy*, to which he contributed for many years. Despite being self-taught, Adolf has attained a very high standard as an airbrush artist and worked on both the book and TV production of Sagan's *Cosmos*, for which he won an award. In addition, he has supervised visual and sound effects for films, videos and musical stage plays, is a composer of seven symphonies and several tone-poems, and a model-builder. He is writing several books, some of which are in collaboration with Mark Paternostro and David J. Eicher.

Adolf's major work to date (and the last seven years in the making) is a comprehensive series on particle physics, cosmology and the evolution of the universe. He has worked for several planetariums, and his work is owned by Carl Sagan, James Oberg, Gentry Lee and many others. His long-term plans include establishing a 'Cosmic History' museum.

being received by great antennae on Earth. The actual power of the craft's transmitter is unbelievably low, and the probe does not have colour cameras. A rotating filter selects the colour or wavelength required: in red, blue, green or ultraviolet.

So the billions of 'bits' (binary digits) which make up the image have to be recorded, then manipulated and enhanced by computer. In the case of Jupiter and Io, certain meteorological or geological features were made to stand out in this way. Space artists understand this quite well and make their own decisions when creating a painting, just as the scientists do with their digital information, on how to portray the celestial body in question. In general, it is probably true to say that the artists' versions are more trustworthy!

The colours of Io (see pages 168, 169 and cover) are due to sulphur, which can be found in various 'allotropes'; it is pale yellow at low temperatures, but changes through orange and red to brown and black when heated, retaining that colour when it cools. The most exciting aspect about Io is that it has *active* volcanoes. According to one theory, these are caused by sulphur dioxide (SO_2) boiling when it contacts sulphur, even though at temperatures far below zero. Expanding greatly in volume below Io's crust, it forces its way to the surface in a rocket-like blast, forming the typical volcanic 'plume' — a parasol-like jet extending as high as 155 miles/250 km into space, its material falling back to the surface.

The energy for all this activity is tidal. Jupiter exerts a massive

gravitational pull on Io's interior, but the moon is locked in place between other Galilean satellites and the energy is converted into heat. Io must have turned completely inside out since its formation.

Meanwhile, back on Jupiter there is also much activity. Despite its size, Jupiter rotates in 9 hours 51 minutes — faster than any other planet — and the equator rotates 5 minutes more rapidly than the temperate regions. As a result, there are powerful winds at the boundaries between the darker, reddish-brown 'belts' and the lighter 'zones'. There are jet streams, moving

Artist Profile

ALAN GUTIERREZ

Alan Gutierrez was born in 1958 and has a Bachelor of Fine Arts degree from the College of Design, Pasadena. He lives in Sedona, Arizona.

While doing research for a college assignment, he came in contact with SF magazines, and in 1977 changed his major from civil engineering. He produced his first artwork in the same year

and made his first professional sale in 1981. He works in gouache, oils or acrylic, and has done cover art for books by Asimov, Bob Shaw and others. His major work to date is 'Legions of Power'.

Alan is primarily a science-fiction artist, but his painting 'Into the Forge of God' (above), which appeared on the cover of a book of almost the same title by Greg Bear, has been widely acclaimed by space art fans. It shows the Galileo probe descending into the clouds of Jupiter around sunset; it will relay its findings via the orbiter, which will also explore the Jovian moons, of which Io and Ganymede are visible here.

at up to 400 ft/150 m per second. And there are other spots, both whitish and dark, which may have their 'roots' deep in Jupiter's fluid interior. In addition, there are constant 'superbolts' of lightning (which can often be seen on the night side of the planet in artists' renderings). It may be the action of these on the methane and ammonia in the hydrogen atmosphere that creates yellow and orange organic polymers, giving Jupiter its characteristic colours. Above we see the Galileo probe descending into this weird region.

Ringworlds One other surprise of the Voyager/Jupiter encounter was that rings were discovered for the first time. They are thin and ribbon-like, and were best seen when backlit, with Voyager 2 in the planet's shadow. Until then, Saturn was thought to be unique in having a beautiful system of gleaming rings. For many years textbooks depicted Saturn as having three rings: the bright Ring A, a duller Ring B (with the dark Cassini Division between them) and the faint, transparent Ring C, also known as the Crêpe Ring. Voyager revealed literally thousands. Don Dixon, who created the spectacular vision of the rings on page 117, has written and illustrated his own book, *Universe* (1981).

Alex Schomburg's rendering (below) was accurate for its time because the planet was based on the Pioneer 11 images of 1979. The resolution was not as good as Voyager's, but it showed the rings, for the first time, not brightly illuminated by the Sun but backlit. Pioneer also detected additional rings.

As with Jupiter, it is Saturn's natural satellites that have been, and still are, of interest to artists. Both Rudaux and Bonestell painted them, the latter's favourite being Titan (opposite), which had been shown to have an atmosphere (thought to be the only moon in the Solar System to possess one). This is because Titan is even larger than the planet Mercury. (Ganymede and Neptune's moon Triton are now known to be slightly larger.) Bonestell therefore painted the sky blue. When I was working with Patrick Moore on *Challenge of the Stars* (1972) I did some research and found

Above: Drawing by **Jack Coggins.**
(Pages 112–13) 'Into the Forge of God' by **Alan Gutierrez** *(acrylics, courtesy of the artist). The Galileo probe descends by parachute into the multi-coloured cloud canyons of giant Jupiter, relaying its findings to an orbiter until crushed by the pressure of the atmosphere. The moons, Io (left) and Ganymede, are visible.*
Left: 'Saturn Probe' by **Alex Schomburg** *(courtesy of the artist). Although primarily a science-fiction artist, Schomburg always used the latest information from space probes when creating artwork.*
Right: 'Saturn from Titan' by **Chesley Bonestell.** *When this was painted, it was known only that Titan had an atmosphere, thought to be mainly of methane, so that the sky would be blue.*
(Page 116) Two views of Saturn seen from its moon Iapetus, from which its rings may be clearly seen — not as a straight line, like the moons which orbit in the same plane. Top: This view is by **Michael Carroll** *(1984, acrylics, 14 × 18 in/355 × 457 mm). Bottom: 'Eclipse from Iapetus' by* **Don Dixon** *(acrylics, 11 × 18 in/280 × 457 mm). Iapetus has a bright side and a dark side due to ices on one and either dark rocks or organic deposits on the other.*

Artist Profile

MICHAEL W. CARROLL

Michael Carroll was born in 1955 and has a Bachelor of Fine Arts degree from Colorado State University. He lives in San Diego, California.

His influences were Salvador Dali, Bonestell, Corot, Monet, Edward Hopper — and *Challenge of the Stars*. His father was an aerospace engineer and his parents taught him a love of nature, 'of which the cosmos is certainly an extension'. His first space art, in 1969, depicted a scene from Apollo 8, which subsequently won a newspaper art contest. His first professional work was a poster series for a games company. He counts good illustration as fine art, but adds that about 35 per cent of his work has to be for purely commercial purposes.

Mike's work appears in several books, including *Comet* (1985), *The Universe and Beyond, Beyond Spaceship Earth* (1987), *Mars 1999* (1987) and *Race to Mars* (1988). In addition, it appears in many magazines, such as *Astronomy* and *Ad Astra*; he also writes his own articles and has done some film production art. His major work to date is a series of paintings on a manned Mars settlement, and a series on the Book of Revelations.

He works in acrylics, with some airbrush and pencil, and is currently Staff Artist for the Reuben H. Fleet Space Theater in San Diego. His work was exhibited at 'Planetfest' (1981), 'Other Worlds' (1985–88), 'Space Future Forum' (Moscow, 1987) and other IAAA events. In addition to space art, he enjoys painting realistic historical subjects: architecture, castles, ziggurats, pyramids, biblical scenes and Earthly landscapes. His work is owned by several prominent astronomers and scientists, and he says, 'As space becomes perceived as a real place, space art will become more accepted as a genre'.

Chesley Bonestell

On pages 117 and 118 are two views of the magnificent rings of Saturn from above its cloud layers. Page 117: 'Cassini Division' by **Don Dixon** (detail, 1980, acrylics, 12 × 18 in/305 × 457 mm, from his book Universe. Left: 'Saturnian Night' by **John R. Foster.** Above: 'Buoyant Titan Station' by **Michael Carroll** (15 × 22 in/380 × 560 mm).

Artist Profile

JOHN R. FOSTER

Born in 1957, John Foster had some art school training but is basically self-taught. He lives in Portland, Oregon.

He was inspired by seeing the films *2001* and *Silent Running*, and by seeing the work of Bonestell and Pesek in books and in *National Geographic*. He started drawing at the age of ten, and made his first painting when he was 15. He was first published in a local magazine, and regards himself as equally fine artist and illustrator. He also finds time for photography.

John's work has appeared in *Astronomy* and its calendar (1986 and 1990), and *Sky and Telescope*. He is contributing work to Asimov's 'Library of the Universe' series. His major work to date is a painting entitled 'Valles Marineris'. He paints in acrylics, using spraygun, airbrush and brushwork.

He has produced panoramas and sequences for the Kendall Planetarium since 1983, and also does work for other planetariums, working with their special effects staff. Exhibitions include 'Images of the Universe' at Iowa State University (1986), 'Art of the Cosmos', at the University of California (1987), and 'Dialogues . . .', the IAAA travelling show. He enjoys painting wilderness landscapes, SF, figures and underwater scenes. He hopes to produce a book combining artwork and photography.

that methane in quantity appears greenish, so that is how I painted Titan's sky. By the time of the second edition (*New Challenge of the Stars*, 1978) I had to re-paint it. I kept the same composition, but now the sky was a reddish 'smog' with Saturn briefly visible, and an 'ice volcano' was shown replenishing the hydrogen atmosphere and ejecting 'lava' consisting of liquid methane, ammonia and water.

This was according to a theory put forward by Carl Sagan. But by the time Pioneer and Voyager had sent back their data, artists had to revise their ideas yet again. Michael Carroll illustrates a modern version (above). Titan's sky, like that of Mars, has taken on an orange hue. The atmosphere is composed mainly of molecular nitrogen with some methane, and the temperature in the clouds of Titan is around minus 193°C; the intensity of sunlight is around one per cent of Earth's. (Fortunately, our eyes adapt to low light, so there is no need for an artist's visualization to be dim and murky.)

Later hypotheses and even laboratory experiments by Sagan and others indicate that the clouds may be composed of a reddish-brown organic material known as 'tholin', which is produced when an atmosphere of nitrogen and methane is irradiated by ultraviolet light. Latest theories suggest a reddish ocean of liquid ethane about ½ mile/1 km deep, with islands covered by a dark, organic, tar-like 'snow' that has drifted down from the haze layer high above. But erupting ammonia-water volcanoes are still a possibility, while Ron Miller has suggested a clear area, dubbed the 'Bonestellosphere', above the red clouds.

The Twin Blue Giants The two remaining gas giants, Uranus and Neptune, are very similar in size — around 30,000 miles/50,000 km in diameter, with Uranus being slightly the larger. In March 1977, when Uranus occulted (passed in front of) a star in the constellation of Libra, the star was dimmed several times *before and after* the actual occultation. This was the first proof that Uranus, like Jupiter and Saturn, possesses a set of rings. Voyager confirmed this in 1986. They are composed of dark material, unlike Saturn's which are icy, and there are nine in all.

The most unusual fact about Uranus is its axis. Unlike most worlds, which spin upright like a top, Uranus 'rolls' around its orbit with its equator inclined 98 degrees. Its moons' orbits are inclined by the same angle. Swiss artist Stefan Blaser painted his scene on Umbriel before the Voyager fly-by, and has placed the constellations in their correct positions so that the angular diameter of Uranus (about 11 degrees) can be judged.

French artist Jean-Michel Joly (who works closely with astronomer Jean-Louis Heudier) painted Miranda after the fly-by, so knew that this moon possesses the most spectacular ice-cliffs. As the closest moon, Miranda has an angular diameter of over 23 degrees, but this must be seen as a 'wide-angle' shot.

Artist Profile

JEAN-MICHEL JOLY

Jean-Michel Joly was born in 1948 and attended the École Nationale des Beaux Arts in Paris. He lives in Saint Étienne, France.

He has worked with astronomer Jean-Louis Heudier of Calern Observatory since 1977, when he had to prepare a science exhibit for him. The exhibit was entitled 'L'Astronomie dans la Ville'. He considers himself to be 75 per cent artist, 25 per cent illustrator.

Jean-Michel's work appears regularly in the magazines *Ciel et Espace, Figaro, Le Point, Nice Matin* and *Le Progrès*. He has produced illustrations for the Cappelle le Grande planetarium at Saint Étienne, and also makes excellent sculptures.

In addition to 'L'Astronomie de la Ville', his work has appeared in the exhibitions 'Terre!' (1979), 'Horizons Mathématiques' (1979), 'Halley' (1985), and others. His work is also in private collections, including that of Jean-Louis Heudier (who organized a festival at Nice to commemorate Apollo in July 1989). Asked for his aims and objectives, Jean-Michel replied, 'Citius, altius, fortius' (Quicker, higher, stronger).

(Pages 120–1) Right: 'Uranus from Umbriel' by **Stefan Blaser** (courtesy of Uwe Luserke, Vega Agency, Friolzheim, West Germany). Below: 'Uranus from Miranda' by **Jean-Michel Joly** (acrylics, 19 3/4 × 63 in/500 × 1600 mm, © 1987).

On this and the next spread are four quite different views of Neptune's major moon, Triton, last port of call of Voyager 2 in August 1989. Left: By **Arthur Gilbert** (1988, acrylics on canvas board, courtesy of the artist) with the Sun setting among reddish clouds and spectacular ice peaks. Above: In 'Triton Sea' (oils, 19 3/4 × 55 in/500 × 1400 mm, © 1987), **Jean-Michel Joly** painted Neptune, with its (presumed) ring, reflected in a lake of liquid nitrogen, with methane/water icebergs (similar to those shown in Michael Carroll's version of Titan on page 119). Right: **Joel Hagen's** scene is more romantic in nature, but no less plausible — until close-up images are obtained . . .

Pages 124–5: 'The Frozen Plains of Triton' by **Michael Carroll** (1988, acrylics, 22 × 30 in/560 × 762 mm, courtesy of the artist). Being pre-Voyager, this was based on data which seemed to indicate polar caps on Triton, with a thin atmosphere containing some orange haze layers. Triton's strange orbit indicates a violent past which may have given rise to rifts and canyons as shown here (based on a rift valley in Iceland). There may even be volcanism.

Artist Profile

JOEL HAGEN

Joel Hagen was born in 1948 and has a BA in anthropology. He lives in Oakdale, California.

Bonestell's work excited him while in the sixth grade, since which he has been fascinated by the prospect of mankind moving out into space. His first space paintings were done in 1981 and published in the same year. He does not like distinctions between fine art and illustration: 'I paint, I sculpt, I make things. That's it.' (For the record, Bonestell insisted that *he* was purely an illustrator....)

Joel's work was included in *The Planets* (1985), an unusual collection of essays, speculation and artwork by leading exponents, *The Search for Extraterrestrial Intelligence* (1986) and *Space — the Next 25 Years* (1987).

He also paints SF subjects, does computer art and animation, and sculpts 'alien fossils', which may find their way into his artwork. He is 'exploring a more personal style, still firmly based on planetary geology'. While his space-related work is often 'realistic', it does have an attractively different and somewhat surrealistic approach.

During 1989 many space artists were eagerly awaiting the final Voyager fly-by of Neptune, Uranus's blue-green twin. Telescopes reveal only two satellites, the large Triton (seen here in four quite different artists' interpretations), which orbits in a retrograde direction at a very high inclination of 160 degrees, and the tiny Nereid. More moons, and a ring, were predicted.

To the Stars

From Red Dwarfs to Black Holes

6

The possible planets of other stars allow artists more freedom of imagination than the planets of our Solar System. We cannot examine them with a telescope (indeed, only indirect evidence, such a 'wobble' in a star's movements, suggests that they are there at all), and we have not yet launched an intentional probe to a star. Voyager I, after leaving the Solar System in 1990, is heading towards the constellation Ophiuchus, which also happens to contain Barnard's Star, a small 'red dwarf'. This is the destination of *Daedalus*, subject of a BIS design study to investigate the feasibility of a simple, unmanned star-probe. In Ron Miller's painting (below) its ionization trail is seen from the surface of the outermost planet, Pluto. Also in the sky is Pluto's relatively large moon, Charon. But Pluto itself is only around 1800 miles/3000 km in diameter itself, and both may once have been satellites of Neptune. Something very strange and cataclysmic seems to have occurred in the outer Solar System.

Travel to the stars is several orders of magnitude more difficult than reaching our own planets. Even at the speed of light (186,000 mps/300,000 kps), which is probably unattainable, it would take over four years to reach the nearest star, Proxima Centauri (pages 134–5). *Daedalus* is a two-stage vehicle, with a primary engine some 400 ft/120 m in diameter generating its thrust from 'micro-pellets' of deuterium and helium-3, expelled into a magnetic field and providing 250 miniature nuclear explosions per second — a nuclear pulse-jet.

Below: *'Daedalus Launch'* by **Ron Miller** *(acrylics, courtesy of the artist). A group of astronauts watch from Pluto, outer planet of our Solar System, as the ion-trail of star-probe* Daedalus *streaks across the black sky in which hangs the large, close moon Charon.*

Right: 'Daedalus' by **Greg A. West** (1981, acrylics, 16 × 20 in/406 × 508 mm, courtesy of the artist) shows the second stage of the unmanned star-probe as it passes close to a red-lit, cratered planet of Barnard's Star. Unable to brake, it would flash right through the system in under ten hours, dropping small probes.

Right, below: 'Asteroid Ark' was painted by **Alex Schomburg** for the January 1985 cover of Amazing when he was almost 80 years old. The subject of a hollowed-out asteroid being fitted with motors and used as a 'generation starship' (only the descendants of the original crew arriving) was one that he had covered several times before; this is probably his best version. (Courtesy of the artist and Chroma, 1986)

Artist Profile

GREGORY A. WEST

Greg West was born in 1950, 'finished high school and attended college sporadically, but earned no degrees'. He lives in Charlotte, North Carolina.

Greg began drawing space pictures in elementary school, between the ages of six and eight. Like many other artists, he saw Bonestell paintings in *Life* magazine at the age of ten or 12. At 13 he started reading Robert Heinlein. His first painting was published in 1978, and he has done covers for *New Destinies III* and *IV, Beginnings, Ardneh's World* and *Twice in Time* (all 1988).

As this list suggests, Greg does produce more SF and fantasy-orientated work than astronomical, but he is becoming a leading exponent of the surrealistic school of space art. Both his realistic and surrealistic types are represented in this book.

His work is included in 'Dialogues . . .', the IAAA travelling exhibition. His ambition, he says, is to reach a position where he can paint full time.

Left: 'Outbound' by **Doug McLeod** (1988, acrylics, 14 × 19 in/356 × 482 mm, courtesy of the artist) depicts an interstellar vehicle beginning its journey to one of the nearer stars. It is propelled by a Daedalus-type fusion-drive engine.

'Barnard's Planet' by **Joe Tucciarone** (acrylics on canvas board, 16 × 20 in/406 × 508 mm, courtesy of the artist). A view of the gas giant planet which is suspected to orbit Barnard's Star, hanging in the sky of a cratered satellite. This system is six light years away from ours.

Artist Profile

DOUGLAS McLEOD

Doug McLeod lives in Webster, Texas, and gained a Bachelor of Aerospace Engineering degree, with honours, from Georgia Institute of Technology. He interned at JIAFS — a joint institute between George Washington University and NASA Langley Research Center. He is self-taught as an artist.

He worked at Johnson Space Center as a software engineer ('video games for astronauts') for four years before turning to illustration full time. Influences include Bonestell ('of course'), McCall, Rawlings, Hudson, Syd Mead and Jim Burns. His first space painting, 'an awful rendition of a planet', was produced towards the end of 1985; a month before he had impulsively left his job to become an 'artist'. He is still an illustrator, but hopes to find the time to expand into the fine arts too.

Doug has prepared eight illustrations, including a cover, for Asimov's 'Library of the Universe' series. These, he says, reflect the style he intends to pursue: 'realistic impressions of nature plus technology in the future'. Peter Diamandis, co-founder of the International Space University, owns his 'Space for All Nations' original, prepared for a 1988 SEDS Conference poster.

He also paints science fiction and horror subjects, as well as 'some airbrushed abstract expressionism on the side', and 3-D stained-glass sculpture. In 1988 he began to work with Pat Rawlings and the Eagle Engineering Group (see page 57) and he plans to continue producing illustrations for NASA, but also to break into SF to explore wilder, more visionary future alternatives.

Artist Profile

JOSEPH M. TUCCIARONE

Born in 1953, Joe Tucciarone has an MS in physics, with a minor in astrophysics. He lives in Cocoa, Florida.

His interest in art and astronomy dates back to the age of ten when Bonestell inspired him to try his own hand at space art. The first time he was paid for it was at the age of 19, for the Planetarium in Youngstown, Ohio. He considers his major work to date to be a painting entitled 'New Moon', which appeared on the back cover of the January/February 1989 issue of *Planetary Report*.

Joe teaches astronomy at Daytona Beach Community College and is staff artist and photographer at the Astronaut Memorial Hall Planetarium in Cocoa, Florida. He has also worked for the Memphis Museum Planetarium and Ethyl Planetarium in Richmond, Virginia, in the same capacity.

He took part in the 'Other Worlds' 1985–88 exhibition, 'Art of the Cosmos' at the Lawrence Livermore Hall of Science (1987), and is included in 'Dialogues …', the IAAA's travelling show from 1989. He works in acrylics, in both brush and airbrush, on canvas board, and aims 'to produce fine (space) art, not just hard, technical, hardware-oriented space art'.

The second stage, with its 500-tonne payload, would reach a speed of about 14 per cent that of light, and after 47 years would release ten or 20 highly sophisticated robot probes in the vicinity of Barnard's Star. It would be another six years before its signals would be received on Earth for analysis. This was, naturally, only a design study, but it is worth mentioning that in 1939 the British Interplanetary Society published a design study for a manned vehicle to the Moon. It contained many features that were incorporated into the Apollo project some 30 years later.

There is not room here to mention all the alternative proposals for star travel. There are ramscoops, collecting interstellar hydrogen as fuel, the Enzmann Starship, using a giant snowball of frozen deuterium (collected from the atmosphere of Jupiter), photon drives and anti-matter. One method, which is actually quite inexpensive, has captured the interest of space artists recently — the light sail. Under the guidance of scientist and SF author Dr David Brin, Project Solar Sail has gathered other authors (including Arthur C. Clarke), artists and scientists to produce a book to promote interest in the idea of sailing to the stars.

We may expect practical experiments in near-Earth space quite soon on sails made of thin, reflective metallic or plastic film which can be propelled by the pressure of radiation from the Sun — or other stars. For starflight, these would be hundreds of kilometres across, towing payloads at the end of fine,

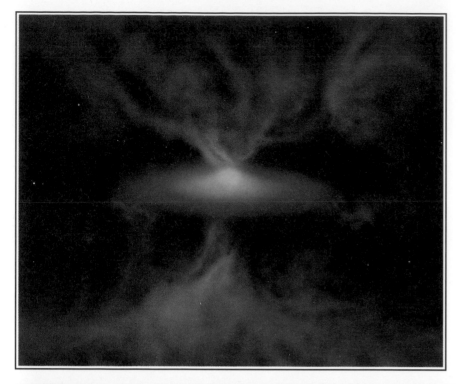

Artist Profile

DOROTHY SIGLER NORTON

Dorothy, who is also known by her maiden name of Dorothy Sigler, was born in 1945 and has a Bachelor of Fine Arts degree from Washington University and a Master of Arts from the University of Iowa. She lives in Bend, Oregon, where she works with her husband, O. Richard Norton, who is President of Science Graphics, a company well known for its teaching slides.

She saw Bonestell's work in *The World We Live In* (a book made from the *Life* series) in 1952, but did her first space art only in 1979, after working for many years as an abstract painter. She says, 'I'm a scientific illustrator mainly (but never completely).' She has illustrated a textbook on human anatomy, *Human Structure* (1987), and is working on a histology text. Her astronomical work has appeared in *Planetary Report* and in Science Graphics slides.

She works in airbrushed acrylics and has produced illustrations for Flandrau Planetarium, Tucson, Arizona. She has done a lot of production work, landscapes, portraits and even cartoons, and now does much 'straight' scientific illustration — medical, biological and geological — some pen and ink. She also paints extinct animals, but 'space art is becoming more important to me'.

(Pages 130–1) 'Gas Giant' by **Ron Miller** (1987, acrylics, from Cycles of Fire, courtesy of the artist). This could almost be the scene from the gas giant planet in the last picture, looking through its clouds towards the moon, which eclipses its distant sun (though not a red one).

Left: 'Infant Solar Disc' by **Dorothy Sigler Norton** (courtesy Science Graphics). A very early stage in the formation of a planetary system; gas and dust surround the protostar, forming a rotating disc from which the planets eventually form by accretion (see pages 68–9). Below: 'Beta Pictoris' by **Mark Maxwell** (1988, acrylics on masonite, 14 × 19 in/355 × 487 mm, courtesy of the artist). In 1981 new techniques in astrophotography revealed a disc-shaped ring of material around this star. Hollow regions may indicate that planets are forming. Right: 'Red Giant' by **Ed Buckley** (1964, enamels, courtesy of the artist) shows explorers on the moon of a planet of a massive red star.

(Pages 134–5): 'Planet of Proxima Centauri' by **David A. Hardy** (1989, acrylics, 18½ × 30 in/470 × 760 mm). A hypothetical planet of our nearest stellar neighbour in space — a red dwarf. In order for liquid water to exist, the planet would need to have an orbital period of about ten days. The other two members of the Alpha Centauri system are visible as bright white stars. (Stars are not really red or blue; their basically white radiation is tinged according to temperature.)

very strong cables. Or, as proposed by Dr Robert L. Forward, they could be propelled by banks of powerful lasers placed in orbit round the Sun and drawing energy from it.

Human ingenuity is stretched to the limit by projects such as this, and mankind needs such challenges. However, before we travel to other stars we need to know that there are planets around them on which to land.

There are two main methods by which we can detect another possible planetary system. One is if a star has a companion which does not glow, so is not itself a star, but is large enough to cause a perturbation in the star's motion through space. The only planet large enough to do this is a gas giant, similar to but even bigger than Jupiter. If it is more than 80 times more massive it would begin to shine as a star; below that threshold it might become a 'brown dwarf', still radiating heat left over from its formation billions of years ago.

The other method uses infra-red radiation. A process known as 'infra-red speckle interferometry' obtains as much detail as possible from small objects by taking a series of short exposures. The images are then processed by computer. The first planet, or brown dwarf (this is a grey area for terminology) to be discovered by this method was Van Biesbroeck 8B, in 1984. Even the Hubble Space Telescope would have difficulty in seeing it, as it is six million times fainter in visible light than in infra-red. None the less, telescopes in space do offer the best hope of finding other planetary systems.

It must be said that there is still controversy among astronomers on the existence of brown dwarfs, but artists certainly enjoy portraying them. Meanwhile, the Infra-red Astronomical Satellite (IRAS) has at least produced evidence of planetary systems in the process of formation. It discovered discs of dust around several nearby stars and, while not 'proof' in strictly scientific terms, there is a high probability that these do represent an early stage in the formation of planetary systems.

On pages 132–3 Dorothy Sigler portrays a forming infant solar disc and protostar inside a dark nebula of dust and gas. Material falls in through the rotational poles of the disc, while the rapid rotation of the contracting star throws material from the star's equator into the disc. Below, Mark Maxwell visualizes swarms of solid particles tightly orbiting Beta Pictoris, one of the systems detected by IRAS. Scottish artist Ed Buckley imagines a much later stage in a star's evolution — a red giant. Our own Sun originated as shown here, five billion years ago, and will end up as a red giant in another five billion years.

Before leaving IRAS, it is worth mentioning an interesting project undertaken by Dutch artist Peter Coene (it is difficult to illustrate). In 1986 a large exhibition called Space '86 was held in Utrecht in the Netherlands. Thanks largely to the efforts of Frederick C. Durant, III in the USA liaising with Dr Chriet Titulaer in the Netherlands, several of the US, European and Soviet artists in this book exhibited works there.

In a planetarium dome made by the Philips company, Peter Coene produced a work entitled 'IRAS, Magnificent IRAS'. The original is now lost for all time, as it consisted of an image of the Milky Way and the Orion

'Hibernating Lifeform' by **Pamela Lee** *(1987, acrylics, from Cycles of Fire, courtesy of the artist). This creature hibernates through a long winter, waiting for the brief spring it will enjoy when its planet, caught on an elliptical orbit between two stars, at last swings close to its primary star and the temperature rises above freezing point.*

Nebula as 'seen' by IRAS, built up in airbrush on an area of about 860 sq ft/ 80 sq m. The dome was dismantled after the exhibition. (Also part of the exhibition, but away from it, was a full-size cardboard replica of Saturn 5 against a church tower in Utrecht. This caused some controversy among local residents, but was certainly very effective.)

In the early days of astronomy there appeared to be three main types of object: stars (of which our Sun is one), planets (with their satellites), and nebulae. In addition there were transitory phenomena like 'shooting stars', which we now know to be caused by particles usually no larger than grains of sand burning up in our atmosphere by friction with the air, and comets,

Right: 'Star Flowers and Mountains' by **John R. Foster** (courtesy of the artist). In the stillness of the night glacier-fed waterfalls cascade over precipitous cliffs into a placid mountain lake. But this is not Earth. Like a beautiful star-studded flower, the Great Orion Nebula glows in the sky of this distant world.

Below: 'Orchid Nebula' by **Kim P. Poor** (acrylics, courtesy of the artist and Novagraphics). It is surely no surprise that nebulae are so often likened to flowers, for their gaseous petals unfold and their hot, bright stars give rise to new worlds — and new life — like star-seeds.

which enter our part of the system on huge elliptical or parabolic orbits.

Using only their eyes, observers saw faint, misty patches. If these moved night after night, they were comets that had not yet developed tails (to be pushed, like a solar sail, by light pressure as they approached the solar fires). But if they remained in the same place relative to the other stars, they were all taken to be patches of gas. It was not until photography could be married with astronomy, and long exposures could be used on these objects (with the telescope driven to compensate for Earth's rotation) that they were found to belong to two different categories. One type is indeed a nebula — a vast cloud of tenuous gas and dust such as the Orion Nebula, illuminated by bright stars within it and often containing dark globules which are the birthplace of new stars and stellar systems. The other is quite different. It does not even belong to our own galaxy, for it is a galaxy itself — an island universe containing perhaps 100 billion stars.

The advent of colour photography and new, high-speed emulsions brought a new dimension to the photography of nebulae. The stars embedded in nebulae are blue-white and very hot, their radiation rich in ultraviolet and X-rays. Short wavelengths like this excite the atoms of gas in a nebula, which then re-radiate at their own wavelengths. The main gas is hydrogen, which has a characteristic red-pink glow; oxygen appears green, and neon is orange-red. Other gases present are nitrogen, argon, sulphur and chlorine. There are also dark nebulae, usually seen because they blot out the light of stars or bright nebulae behind them. They seem to form dark 'lanes' in the star-clouds of the Milky Way, and have no stars within them to excite their gases.

Artists are naturally attracted to such spectacular and colourful objects, as pages 138–9 show. But, if the early astronomers could see only faint patches of mist, with no discernable colour, would they really be so attractive if we could see them in close-up with the naked eye? The answer has to be 'No', strictly speaking, for the actual level of light given out by emission nebulae is very low. So is, for that matter, the level of light from a spiral galaxy seen from a distance of a couple of hundred thousand light years. (Galaxies exist in various forms, including elliptical, irregular and spiral. Each shape represents a different stage in their evolution.)

However, this apparent dimness does not mean that space artists are lying, or even being over-imaginative in their colourful depictions. As seen earlier with Jupiter and Io, colours can change according to the manner in which they are observed or recorded, and the space artist often sees him or herself as a camera, taking photographs where no photographs can yet be taken. If a camera containing colour film were set up on a planet at a suitable distance from a picturesque nebula and other bright objects were visible, such as a sunlit landscape or even a moon in the sky, then the exposure required for those objects would render the nebula almost invisible. But if the nebula were the only source of illumination, then a longer exposure would be required and the colours would be as artists depict them, even when reflected on a landscape as in John Foster's evocative scene.

Artist Profile

KAZUAKI IWASAKI

Kazuaki Iwasaki was born in 1935 of Japanese parents living in China, returned to Japan in 1946, and now lives in Osaka.

At the age of 14 he developed an interest in painting, as well as astronomical observation, and he continues to observe the stars and planets, believing that astronomical art (as he prefers to call it) must reflect scientific facts and findings. The telescopes he uses are an 8-in/20-cm refractor and a 25-in/65-cm reflector. He says, 'My artwork was the natural consequence of observing heavenly objects and is not a commercial work of illustration. I welcome an association with those artists who share the same idea.' In 1953 he joined the astronomical division of the Asahi Optical (Pentax) Corporation, and in 1958 opened his own design company, Kazuaki Iwasaki Design Co. Ltd. His first book, *This is Cosmos,* was published in 1956.

In 1983 Fred Durant helped him to organize a two-man exhibition of Bonestell and Iwasaki in various Japanese cities for a year. His book *Visions of the Universe* was produced in Japan for Carl Sagan's company, and translated by Shigeru Komori, a personal friend, who also represents the Planetary Society in Japan. Komori says, 'I support a project which will expand the exposure of space art to many people in the world.' Iwasaki's book *Artistic Voyage Through Space and Nature* (with text in Japanese) contains, in addition to astronomical subjects, many delightful renderings of natural history subjects. He has exhibited widely, and has been honoured by the Tokyo Illustrators' Club.

Kazuaki Iwasaki 143

(Pages 140–1) *Two views of our own Milky Way Galaxy: one from outside, one from its very centre. Left: 'Rise of the Milky Way' by* **Kurt C. Burmann** *(1982, acrylics, 30 × 36 in/762 × 915 mm, courtesy of the artist). Our galaxy is surrounded by a halo of 'stray stars', some of which may have planets. Here we see a view from perhaps 200,000 light years. Right: 'Milky Way Nucleus' by* **Adolf Schaller** *(acrylics with airbrush, 20 × 30 in/508 × 762 mm, courtesy of the artist). Seen from the vantage point of a small, rocky planetoid just a few light years away, the nucleus of the Milky Way presents a frightening spectacle. At the core of a swarm of billions of stars is a collection of various collapsed objects — white dwarfs, neutron stars and black holes — whose mutual motions and gravitational/magnetic fields choreograph the bizarre dance of an 'accretion skirt' of gas. The main player is a supermassive black hole, with an estimated mass of between 10 and 100 million times that of the Sun. Gas plunging into it may create a small quasar, rivalling the power output of the rest of the stars in the galaxy.*

Below, left: *'Centaurus A Nebula' by* **Kazuaki Iwasaki** *(water-colour, 18 × 13½ in/456 × 339 mm, courtesy of the artist) is also an exotic object. It is, in effect, an exploding galaxy; an explosion at the centre has blown out a ring of gas, not normally seen in an elliptical galaxy. Radio telescopes reveal large clouds on either side of the galaxy, which emit powerful radio waves generated by the energetic central nucleus.*
Below, right: *'Galactic Jet' by* **Ron Miller** *(1987, acrylics, from Cycles of Fire, courtesy of the artist). Some galaxies emit jets containing a flood of charged atomic particles. Here, such a jet passes through a close 'satellite galaxy', inducing aurorae in the upper atmosphere of the foreground planet near its poles. No life is likely to exist there . . .*

This mention of photography brings up another point: the visibility of stars. In Apollo photographs the sky is totally black; the astronauts said that they could not see stars unless they shielded their eyes from all sources of bright light. And as seen above, photographic film cannot be exposed for the stars without completely over-exposing sunlit objects, or vice versa. So why is it that artists nearly always show stars when depicting space? The answer is quite simple: painters have an advantage over the camera. The stars are there and *can* be seen, and the artist, unlike the photographer (unless the latter does a lot of manipulation in the darkroom), can show them at the same time as other objects.

Kim P. Poor, whose nebula painting is on page 138, is a strong advocate for artists' rights, a past President of the International Association for the Astronomical Arts (IAAA), and runs his own business, Novagraphics, selling fine art prints of space subjects by himself and other artists. He uses the airbrush almost exclusively, as does Japanese artist Kazuaki Iwasaki (page 142). Several volumes of Iwasaki's work have been published, including *Visions of the Universe* (1981) and *Artistic Voyage Through Space and Nature* (1987). His painting of the giant elliptical galaxy Centaurus A, like Ron Miller's of a jet emitted by an active galaxy (both are powerful emitters of radio waves) and Adolf Schaller's of a fantastic black hole at the nucleus of our own galaxy, depict some of the more esoteric objects in the universe. Many can only ever be visited by the imagination. Perhaps. . . .

Space Fantasies
The New Renaissance

'Pangenesis' (left) and 'Triumphal Arch' by **Ludek Pesek** (both acrylics/oils, 23½ × 15¾ in/600 × 400 mm, courtesy of Space Art International and the artist). These are examples of Pesek's 'cosmic surrealism', in which he juxtaposes familiar objects — flowers, butterflies, buildings — with astronomical scenes. Close scrutiny is advised.

(Pages 146–7) 'Twin Universes' (left) and 'Blue Planet' by **Beth Avary** (acrylics, courtesy of the artist). The premises of 'astrosurrealism' also often require the juxtaposing of elements of terrestrial (familiar) and astronomical elements, yet the result is quite different. The galaxy and the underwater scene depict an exquisite alien world; the viewer's interpretation is a personal matter.

Artist Profile

LUDEK PESEK

Ludek Pesek was born in 1919 and is a citizen of Stäfa, Switzerland. He attended the Academy of Fine Arts.

He became interested in astronomy and space art at the age of 19, inspired by a telescope at school and a book by Lucien Rudaux. (Indeed, Pesek's landscapes suggest the influence of Rudaux, rather than Bonestell.) He first produced his own work at that time, and his first publications were *The Moon and Planets* (1963) and *Our Planet Earth* (1967). He thinks of himself as 50:50 illustrator and fine artist.

As mentioned earlier, his work first reached US readers through the *National Geographic Magazine*. Previous to the Mars article he had painted 15 scenes for an article called 'Journey to the Planets' in August 1970. In 1967 Ludek wrote his first science-fiction novel, *Log of a Moon Expedition* (illustrated in black and white). Another, *The Earth Is Near* won Prize of Honour in Germany in 1971. It was published in the UK and USA in 1974. He illustrated *Space Shuttles* in 1976.

He worked with writer Peter Ryan on several slim books for children: *Journey to the Planets* (1972), *Planet Earth* (1972), *The Ocean World* (1973) and *UFOs and Other Worlds*, (1975); he later worked with the same author on the large-format *Solar System* (1978). He also illustrated the excellent *Bildatlas des Sonnensystems* (1974), with text (in German only) by Bruno Stanek. His other publications include a photographic record of Lebanon's historical monuments and natural beauties, and several other novels; one, *Preis der Beute* (Price of a Prey), is about the lives of whalers from old times to the present.

From 1981 to 1985 he produced a series of 35 paintings on 'The Planet Mars', of which two are reproduced here, and a series of 50 paintings, 'Virgin Forests in the USA'. He has produced several 360-degree panoramas for projection in the domes of planetariums at Stuttgart, Winnipeg and Lucerne, and has exhibited in Washington, DC, Boston, Nashville, Stuttgart, Berne, Lucerne, Zurich, and other venues. His work is in the collection of the Smithsonian Institution.

*. . . And I have felt A presence that disturbs me with the joy
Of elevated thoughts: a sense sublime Of something far more deeply interfused,
Whose dwelling is the light of setting suns, And the round ocean and the living air . . .*
— 'Lines Composed a Few Miles Above Tintern Abbey' William Wordsworth, 1798

Many space artists are content to render the universe, or space technology, purely in terms of realism and accuracy. This is fine because 'photographs of the unphotographable', as I call them, are very necessary in showing where Man is going in the future. But, as in other areas of art, some feel the need to express a more spiritual or emotional approach to the mysteries of the Cosmos. Many of the Soviet artists have this approach.

Some artists use both a realistic and a more symbolic approach. Ludek Pesek is well known for his highly accurate, if somewhat impressionistic space landscapes; but he also produces what he calls 'cosmic surrealism', as shown here. At first glance these may appear to be quite familiar objects, but

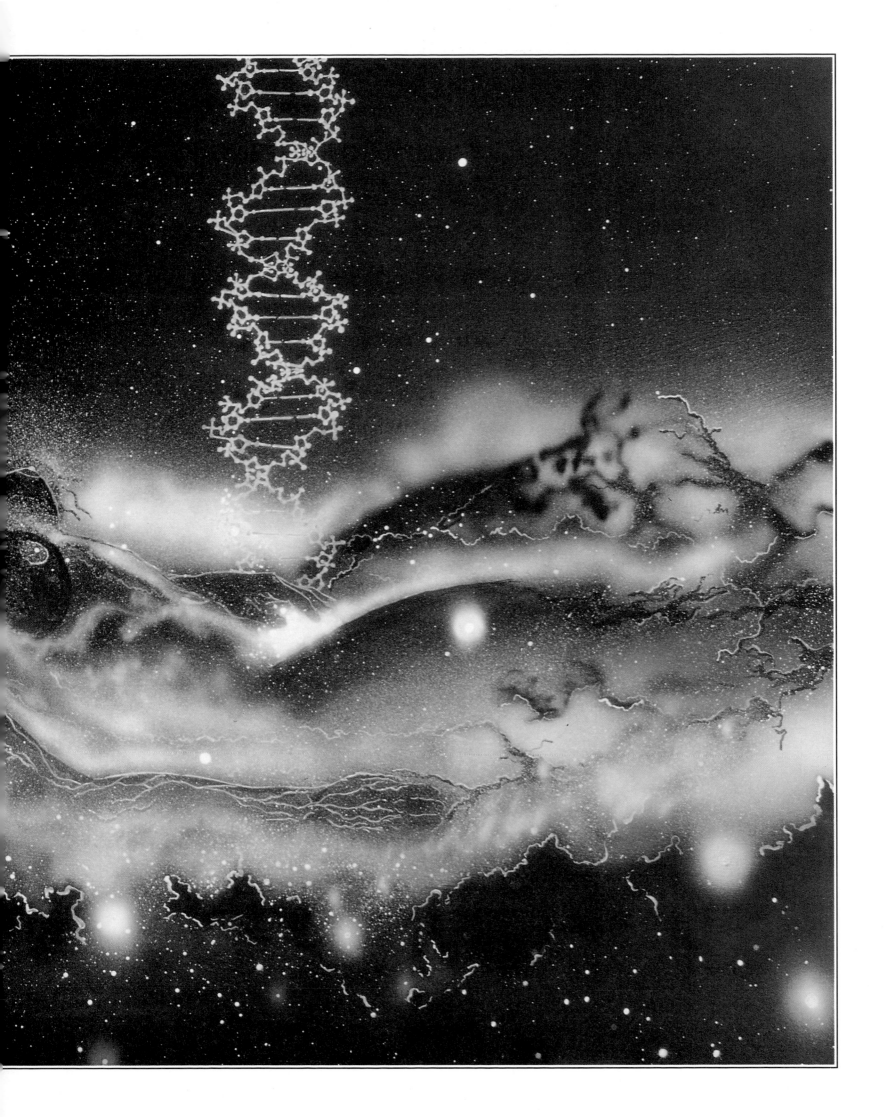

(Pages 148–9) 'Milky Way Woman' by **Jon Lomberg** (acrylics, 20 × 30 in/508 × 762 mm, collection of Professor Frank Drake). The woman in the starfields is announcing her presence to the universe by showing the structure of DNA. This painting was inspired by Frank Drake's transmission of the structure of DNA in his broadcast (to anyone 'out there') from the Arecibo radio telescope in 1974.

Left: 'Curiosity: the Moment of Creation' (1988, acrylics, 34 × 48 in/914 × 1220 mm). Right: 'Bon Voyage: Apprehension' (1988, acrylics, both courtesy of the artist), by **Kara Szathmáry.** (The artist's artistic philosophy is explained on pages 151–2.)

Artist Profile

KARA SZATHMÁRY

Kara Szathmáry was born in 1945 and has a BSc in physics and mathematics from McMaster University (1970), and an MSc in astrophysics from the University of Western Ontario (1972). He also has a DEd (teacher's diploma) from McGill University (1976). He lives in Quebec, Canada.

He is self-taught as an artist, with 20 years of painting experience in oils and acrylics. Apart from Van Gogh (see pages 151–2) his influences were Tom Thompson and the 'Group of Seven' landscape painters in Canada. He produced his first space art in 1969, was first published in 1976, and considers himself a fine artist.

Kara's work appeared in the October 1986 issue of *Sky and Telescope*, and in the *Space Encyclopedia* (1987). He is the inventor of 'Quantum Baseball', which he describes as a Space Age (zero-gravity), card-playing, board and baseball game. Among his major works he lists 'Curiosity: The Moment of Creation' (1984 and 1988) as a large piece, reproduced opposite.

He has taken part in several group and one-man exhibitions, including one at the University of Sherbrooke in Quebec (1988), and was a juror (with Hardy and Avary, all three being included in the exhibition) for the 'Dialogues...' show which opened in Moscow in 1989. He is President of the IAAA, a position he holds until 1992. Kara also paints Earth landscapes and wild flowers, and makes woodcuts. His studies of science and philosophy are reflected in his work.

when one realizes that a vine is growing on an asteroid, or a temple is on the Moon, it can lead to a strange feeling of disorientation.

Beth Avary calls her type of art 'astrosurrealism', a branch of veristic surrealism applied to space art. 'Twin Universes' (page 146), shows a spiral galaxy contrasted with an underwater world. Sea shells have a spiral shape which seems to be a feature of nature at many levels of size and scale. Helmut K. Wimmer also uses a cut-open nautilus shell to represent time, from the beginning to the present, in his painting 'Space, Time, Infinity' (pages 154–5). In Beth Avary's 'Blue Planet' she makes the point that astronomers find the universe to be isotropic (equal in all directions) and homogeneous (made of the same kinds of things throughout). She extends this to suggest that life on other worlds might look similar to our own, while being different in some ways. (Our own planet has produced the most incredibly diverse forms, from human beings to strange 'worms' living around sulphurous vents on the ocean floor in the absence of sunlight.)

Canadian artist Kara Szathmáry began as a scientist, and started to use his talent as an artist to visualize problems in physics. He studied the work of Van Gogh for several years, and from this has gone on to be a leading exponent and proponent of non-representational space art. Of his large painting, 'Curiosity: the Moment of Creation', he says: 'Scientists are like children, examining the details of what has come into their hands. From the Big Bang and the early particle universe, they observe and analyse their world to formulate a relationship and understanding of the space-time events in which they are immersed.' Above, 'Bon Voyage: Apprehension' is really self-explanatory.

In 1988 Kara Szathmáry took over from Kim Poor as President of the IAAA, which is now registered as a non-profit organization. I became Vice-President for Western Europe at about the same time. Szathmáry, writing in the IAAA's journal, *Pulsar*, points out that throughout the Renaissance artists, scientists, philosophers and inventors sat at the Medici table. An artist was extremely well-informed about current ideas — indeed, the artist and scientist were often one and the same person.

The romantic approach to painting was fuelled by the idea that art was a vehicle for personal emotion. In contrast to this, the Impressionists attempted to render an 'impression' of what the eyes see at one particular moment, rather than what the mind knows to be there. As a result, Impressionism was often accused of lacking intellectual content. Post-Impressionistic reaction led to the reintroduction of emotional and symbolic content. Art in the twentieth century went through a radical change fuelled by the rejection of the naturalistic tradition, while at the same time, classical physics was being overturned by the quantum theory and general relativity.

In all the chaos that has gripped science and art in the twentieth century, says Szathmáry, the Space Age finally called out for a grand unification of all art styles as well as science. To 'understand' our place in and relationship to the universe, be it cosmic or atomic, an 'all art menu' must be employed. 'Reality' can be expressed in many ways, but the artist must have genuine ideas to express.

Angela Manno has been described as 'a visionary artist deeply committed to the transformation of human consciousness to a global awareness and collective responsibility for the state of our planet'. Her

Artist Profile

ANGELA MANNO

Angela Manno was born in 1953, has a BA from Bard College, and did graduate studies at San Francisco Art Institute. She lives in New York.

She became interested in space after reading astronauts' accounts (particularly Edgar Mitchell's) of viewing the Earth from space. She is a fine artist and began creating space subjects in 1985. Her work was first published in a six-page spread in *The Artist's Magazine* in February 1986. It has also appeared in *Newsday*, *American Craft* and *Interior, Design*.

Angela is currently compiling an anthology — *Planetary Perspectives* — of essays and interviews with scientists, theologians, futurists and ecologists, to be combined with the artwork from her travelling exhibition, 'Conscious Evolution: The World at One'. This is a collection of 13 mixed-media paintings on the subject of global unity. The details of Angela's technique are described on page 153; she also produces decorative fibre art on silk and cotton.

Her work has been exhibited at the United Nations Pavilion, Expo '86 in Vancouver, and the Association of Space Explorers' Third Planetary Congress in Mexico City (1987). It is owned by Apollo astronaut Edgar Mitchell. She was commissioned by NASA to produce work to commemorate the 29 September 1988 launching of the Space Shuttle *Discovery*, marking the return of the US to manned spaceflight. Using her batik technique, she is creating a series of works inspired by her experiences at the Kennedy Space Center during the launch. Her aim in space art is 'to raise people's consciousness about our place in the universal evolutionary process, and our responsibility for the condition of our planet'.

Below: 'Planetary Citizen' (30 × 27 in/760 × 680 mm) and right: 'Earth Steward' (32 × 36 in/810 × 910 mm, both batik with Xerox, courtesy of the artist) by **Angela Manno**. A unique technique within the field of space art, giving very interesting results — and with an important message.

(Pages 154–5) 'Space, Time, Infinity' by **Helmut K. Wimmer** (poster colours, 18 × 32 in/457 × 813 mm, courtesy of the artist). This was painted originally as an opening spread for a book of the same name. The nautilus shell represents Time, from the dawn of life to the present day, with Man's technological triumphs.

technique is also remarkable, for, unique among space artists, she uses batik processes.

This art-form uses dyes to make patterns on cloth by blocking out certain areas with a colourless wax, which is later removed. She transfers a photocopied colour image, made from her own photographs or retouched NASA images, on to cotton fabric by using a heat source. For 'Planetary Citizen' (left) she quotes astronaut Edgar Mitchell: 'Each man comes back [to Earth] with a feeling that he is no longer only an American citizen; he is a planetary citizen.'

Dr Hans-Ulrich Keller, Director of Stuttgart Planetarium (for which both Pesek and I have produced many 360-degree panoramas) is a keen student of space art, which he prefers to call 'cosmic art'. He divides it into three styles: realistic, fantastic and expressionistic. As an illustration of the growing interest in this art-form, he quotes the number of visitors to exhibitions held at the planetarium — some 3.5 million since 1977. Perhaps because my own exhibition there in 1981 (from which eleven paintings were stolen!) consisted largely of work produced for *Galactic Tours* (1981), a sort of interstellar travelogue with SF writer Bob Shaw, he places my work in the 'fantastic' category, though I think of myself as being a realist. I do, however, on occasion produce quite abstract work, and am currently collaborating with Kara Szathmáry. As a leading exponent of the expressionistic school, Dr Keller cites German artist Walter K. Bulander.

Left, below: 'The Galleon' by **Greg A. West** (acrylics, 15 × 20 in/381 × 508 mm, courtesy of the artist). A ship braving the oceans of space? Again, the viewer's own interpretation is paramount.
Right: 'The Encounter' by **Raymond S. Wilson** (acrylics, 30 × 40 in/762 × 1016 mm, courtesy of the artist). Described by the artist as 'an experimental piece', the author's first impression was of a cosmic wave — hence its positioning with the painting opposite. The reader may have other ideas . . .

(Pages 160–1) 'Earth and Moon' by **Robert André** (acrylics on canvas, 31½ × 23½ in/800 × 600 mm, courtesy of the artist). The painting avoids a traditional approach to the subject in order to show a rather poetic aspect.

Artist Profile

RAYMOND S. WILSON

Raymond Wilson was born in 1939 and obtained a BS degree in commercial art, with a minor in music, from the University of Houston in 1963. He lives in Fort Worth, Texas.

In the early 1960s he worked as a technical illustrator at NASA—MSC Clear Lake, then at General Dynamics in Fort Worth, where he painted F–111 fighter aircraft. He also worked as a freelance illustrator for the *World Book Encyclopedia Science Service*, and contributed to the *World Book Encyclopedia Year Book*. He says that he is 70 per cent illustrator, 30 per cent fine artist.

Raymond works in airbrush, using gouache and acrylic, sometimes with water-colour, and also produces technical illustration in pen and ink. He has a particular interest in airbrushing mechanical objects, and has painted backgrounds for the Museum of Science and History, Fort Worth. His work was exhibited at Dallas Illustrators' Society in 1985.

Space art has always been his first love, although he has not always been able to pursue it. However, he is now promoting space art as a fine art form, and is persuading galleries to hang it, having succeeded at Art à la Carte in Fort Worth.

For the work by Greg A. West, Raymond S. Wilson and Stefan Blaser on pages 156 and 157 I coined the term 'astrosymbolism'. (I'm not sure whether they approve, but when I asked Greg West if he had a name for his type of art he replied, 'Well, gosh, let's call it Martha.') His galleon is certainly a 'space ship', and its symbolism is obvious. The others share a quality that is at least semi-abstract.

Swiss artist Robert André's scene on one of the moons of Saturn (or is it a ringed gas giant in another stellar system?) could be an example of a realistic scene — until one notices the focus of interest among the astronauts. The idea of humans finding an artefact or some other evidence of an alien civilization is an old and exciting one, epitomized perhaps by Clarke's *2001*. The search for extraterrestrial intelligence (SETI) has been going on for many years. The first serious attempt, Project Ozma, was initiated in 1960. The only method that can be used is to 'listen in' to radio wavelengths to determine whether anyone out there is communicating with us or anyone else. Jon Lomberg's 'Milky Way Woman' (pages 148–9) announces her presence to the universe through the structure of her DNA — the key-stone of life.

André's atmospheric painting on pages 160–1 is less marginal in content than his first. He describes it as symbolizing the close historic, as well as mythic, relationship between the Earth and the Moon.

On page 163 are two examples of another unusual and very different style of space art, by Lilika Papanicolaou, a native of Greece. A student of history and astronomy, she works in oils on a very large canvas (perhaps 6 × 8 ft/2 × 2.5 m) applying the vivid colours impasto with a palette knife,

robert andré 7/88

Left, top: 'Project Mercury' by **Joel Hagen** (courtesy of the artist). A collage of images symbolizing the launching of the first American into space.

Left, below: 'Since the Last Time' by **Thomas L. Hunt** (alkyd, 24 × 36 in/610 × 915 mm, © Astronomy magazine, Kalmbach Publishing). Hunt also wrote the article which accompanied this illustration, which shows what happened in the world since Comet Halley's last appearance in 1910. The images are placed along the orbit at points where the comet would have been at the time.

Right: *Two Paintings by* **Lilika Papanicolaou** — top: 'Martian Sunset', bottom: 'Galactic Halo' (both oils with palette knife on canvas, courtesy of the artist and Space Art International). The artist says, 'Space is our century; Cosmos was the theme of pro-Socratian philosophers.'

(Page 164) Top: 'A View to the Future' by **Raymond S. Wilson** (gouache and acrylics, 12 × 26 in/305 × 660 mm, courtesy of the artist). The old house stands in Fort Worth: 'It looks so lost and desolate.' The artist has projected it into the future. Who lives there now?

Below: 'Reflections of Future Past' by **Kurt C. Burmann** (acrylics, courtesy of the artist). The painting gives tribute to the past and future of space exploration, reflected in an eye.

(Page 165) 'The Universe Between' by **Don Dixon** (acrylics, 12 × 20 in/305 × 508 mm, courtesy Berkley Books and the artist). Our planet's primordial beginnings; a human hand reaching for the stars; a picture is worth a thousand words . . .

Artist Profile

LILIKA PAPANICOLAOU

Lilika Papanicolaou was born Maria Efthalia Maris in 1923, Lilika being a childhood nickname. She studied painting in Greek, French and English schools. Her husband, Sophocles, is an economist.

Her first exhibition of space-related art was at the Bodley Gallery, New York, in 1981. Since then her work has appeared in one-woman shows at the Club Financiero Genova, Madrid, the Cathedral Museum, Valletta, Malta, the Lincoln Center, New York, Robert Taylor's Galleries, Houston, Texas, and the National Academy of Sciences, Washington, DC. She has also participated in many collective exhibitions in London, Le Touquet, Geneva and other cities. She won the Silver Cup in Concorzo Internazionale di Pittura and the Grolla d'Oro in 1982 at Treviso, Italy. She also took part in 'Space 86' at Utrecht in 1986, where she appeared on an artists' panel with Andrei Sokolov and David A. Hardy, chaired by Dr Chriet Titulaer.

Lilika is the author of a book entitled *Galaxies*, with introductions by Ian Ridpath, John Man and Dr Paul Murdin, which contains reproductions of her own work. Her paintings are in the private collections of the King and Queen of Spain, the King and Queen of Greece, Lord and Lady Rothermere in London, and several others. She says that the mosaic-like nature of her work represents the quanta (units of energy) in nature, and that her philosophy concerns the light of space. She also produces sculpture and poetry.

165

Left: 'Black Hole' by **Andrei Sokolov** (acrylics, 35½ × 27½ in/ 900 × 700 mm, courtesy of Space Art International). This could almost be said to be an abstract version of Schaller's painting on page 141, with its complex gravitational fields and swirling gases.
Right: 'East Meets West (and Goes to Mars)' by **Jon Lomberg** (acrylics on canvas board, 18 × 24 in/457 × 610 mm, courtesy of the artist). A very clever image that speaks for itself — and for international cooperation.

Artist Profile

STEFAN BLASER

Born in 1963, Stefan Blaser attended the Applied Art School in Berne and was educated as a graphic designer and scientific illustrator. He lives in Rüfenacht, Switzerland.

He was influenced by science-fiction films, television programmes and books about space, and produced his first space art when he was eleven years old. It was first published in 1980. When painting a picture for himself, he considers himself an artist, but when painting commissions, he considers himself an illustrator.

Stefan produced a star map and poster for the Swiss Red Cross, and illustrated Stanek's *Dictionary of Spaceflight*. He uses designers' colours mostly, but also likes acrylic paint and black ink for drawings. He has worked for Stuttgart Planetarium and for the planetarium of the excellent Deutsche Museum in Munich.

His work has been exhibited at the Swiss Astronomical Society in Berne (1984), at the 'Alien Worlds' exhibition in Mannheim, and at the Stuttgart Planetarium (summer 1989). In addition to space art, he produces scientific drawings and illustrations for advertising and publicity material. For the former he works with various scientists. He says, 'I think it is important that people think about our small world and its future.'

Artist Profile

BETH AVARY

Beth Avary was born in 1941 and obtained a Bachelor of Fine Arts degree in painting from California College of Arts and Crafts. She lives in Portola Valley, California.

In 1976 she 'went back to school to round off her education with science and maths — took astronomy — fell in love!' Until the 1988 IAAA Iceland Workshop all her work was surreal ('astrosurrealism', as she calls it); it was first published in the magazine *Magical Blend*. She says she is a fine artist interested in illustration.

She produced the exhibition 'Art of the Cosmos' with the Astronomical Society of the Pacific, and wrote a script to propose a Smithsonian travelling exhibition service. She is Director of Exhibitions for the IAAA and wrote the script for the 'Dialogues . . .' travelling international exhibition, curated by the National Air and Space Museum.

Beth considers her major works to be 'Galactiscape', 'Women at the Edge of Time' and 'Together We Can. . .' (reproduced here, on the final spread; the others are in the travelling exhibition). For 'Together We Can. . .' (also the slogan of the Beyond War Movement) she collected rock samples from Iceland for reference purposes, as well as using Viking photographs of Mars for colour accuracy. The 'world flag' represents a future in which there is a World Federation of Countries. The view is from the western end of the Valles Marineris (page 85). She adds, 'Wouldn't it be wonderful to actually go there and walk around?'

producing a vibrant, mosaic-like texture. Frederick Durant calls her paintings 'bold expressions of the energy, light and mystery of the universe', a description which cannot be bettered. Lilika often paints from the edges inward to the centre, and may work for 12 hours or more at a time, listening to classical music, including Byzantine hymns.

When I first saw Raymond S. Wilson's picture (reproduced at the top of page 164), I gave it the title of 'Gateway to the Universe'. I later received his own title, 'A View to the Future'. It seems that the old house stands in Fort Worth, Texas, and he imagined it still standing far in the future, with a light in its window. Who could be living there? This is perhaps as far from the purist's view of space art as anything in this book — but is Earth not a planet? The other paintings on that spread also encompass the theme of a linked past and future.

One ideal which all space artists seem to share is cooperation, in space *and* on the Earth, between Western nations and the Soviet Union. So on this page appears the abstract 'Black Hole' by Andrei Sokolov, with a painting entitled 'East Meets West' by US artist Jon Lomberg, which speaks for itself.

Alien Landscapes
Finding Other Worlds on Earth

The scene on the cover of this book is impossible! It represents an artist's dream. In his 1949 introduction to *The Conquest of Space*, Willy Ley wrote: '[an artist] would have to sit in a spacesuit at a temperature of minus 150 degrees Fahrenheit and see what his paints would do at that temperature in an

*Above: 'Io Caldera' by **Michael Carroll** (acrylics, 16 × 20 in/406 × 508 mm, courtesy of the artist). This scene was based on a sketch (left) of the volcanic crater Ubehebe in Death Valley, California, during a 1983 IAAA workshop. Several kinds of volcanic activity may exist on Io.*

Below: 'Lava Lake on Io' by **MariLynn Flynn** (1988, acrylics, courtesy of the artist). Mountains on Io may be composed of silicate materials rather than sulphur. Here, a lava flow pours past a silicate mountain into a lake of molten sulphur. A small geyser-like eruption also feeds the lake. Based on the sketch (right) of rhyolite mountains and an obsidian lava flow at Landmannalaugar, Iceland, made during the 1988 workshop, where artists coined the term 'rocks & balls' for this type of space art.

atmosphere consisting mostly of methane gas.' He was writing about Chesley Bonestell's vision of Titan, but the sentiments are much the same for Io. (Of course, by the time an artist *can* go there science may have come up

with suitable media. . . .)

However, space artists do succeed in finding substitutes for other planets. The IAAA has held several workshops: in Death Valley, in Hawaii, in Iceland in 1988 — where, for the first time, US artists were joined by about a dozen Soviet artists, one Canadian and one Brit — and Death Valley again in 1989, also with overseas participants. These venues contain geological analogues of other planets — particularly Mars and Io: volcanic craters and cinder cones, fault valleys and fractures, and so forth.

These last few pages contain a selection of other-worldly scenes which

(Pages 172–3) 'Together We Can . . .' by **Beth Avary** (acrylics, courtesy of the artist). The artist picked a spot on Mars — the Valles Marineris canyon — looked at photographs of it, looked at the rock samples she had brought back from Iceland, and created this painting. And she added a 'world flag' because, 'It would be good for the whole world to be involved in space exploration together as a means of uniting the planet and realizing our common humanity'. Amen.

Right: 'Dave Hardy at Landmannalaugar' — drawing by **Kara Szathmáry**.

Far right: 'Hidden Moon' by **Dennis Davidson** (acrylics, 15¾ × 24 in/400 × 610 mm, courtesy of the artist) was painted during the IAAA Hawaii workshop in March 1986. The artist sat in the steaming caldera of Kilauea Iki on a misty day.
Right, bottom: **Don Davis** painted this realistic Martian panorama from sketches and photos taken during the Death Valley workshop. (Courtesy of the artist)

Below: 'Fault Valley on Mars' by **David A. Hardy** (gouache, 15 × 20 in/380 × 510 mm) was painted from the pen-and-pastel sketch (left). The graben (fault valley) at Thingvellir was reversed from left to right, and the more dramatic features of the cliffs have been exaggerated. The valley floor has been widened and a scree-slope has been added at the bottom for the robotic rover to climb. (The whole production of this painting is followed in even greater detail in Step-by-Step Graphics, March/April 1989.)

Artist Profile

DAVID A. HARDY

Dave Hardy was born in 1936 in Birmingham, England, where he still lives. He is basically self-taught as an artist, but worked in a design studio for several years before becoming freelance in 1965. He is a fellow of the British Interplanetary Society and a member of several space societies, as well as current Vice-President for Western Europe of the IAAA.

Facinated by astronomy from a very early age, his first contact with space art was through *The Conquest of Space* and Arthur C. Clarke's early books. He first produced his own in 1950, and was first published in *Suns, Myths and Men* by Patrick Moore in 1954. This led to a long working relationship with Moore, including about a dozen books (the most important being *Challenge of the Stars* — see page 114) and the TV series *The Sky at Night*. He has also supplied art for other TV programmes, including *Cosmos*, and many books, magazines, SF covers, film production art and advertising. He was nominated for a Hugo Award in 1979, and in 1984 was voted Best European SF Graphic Artist. His technique was featured in the March/April 1989 issue of *Step-by-Step Graphics*, and his work is owned by Arthur C. Clarke, Carl Sagan, Charles Sheffield and Isaac Asimov, among many others. He is also a photographer, and is currently producing computer graphics; a remaining ambition is to do matte art for films.

His first one-man exhibition was at the London Planetarium in 1968 and led to the publication of the first and only fine art space print — 'Stellar Radiance' (1970) — to reach the UK annual 'Top Ten Prints' list. His work was displayed at Expo '88 in Australia. Hardy has also produced many 360-degree panoramas for projection in the London and Stuttgart planetariums. In 1974 he began to write and illustrate his own books, of which there are now six, the major one being *Atlas of the Solar System*. However, he considers his most important work to date to be the one you are now reading.

started life as sketches (also included) made *in situ* in those locations listed above. MariLynn Flynn and Michael Carroll found inspiration for Ionian scenes in Iceland and Death Valley. Dennis Davidson actually sat in the sulphurous steam of a crater in Hawaii to paint 'Hidden Moon'. Don Davis (who has the distinction of having studied under Bonestell, and who has worked on the US Geological Survey) based his panorama of Mars on Death Valley, and I sketched an Icelandic graben (fault valley) to produce my own Martian scene, shown here in four stages of its production.

The advantages of these workshops are several. They give artists an opportunity to meet and exchange notes and tips, and to meet their counterparts from other countries. They are able to study the geology of areas which resemble other planets, and sketch or photograph formations which give authenticity to their work. In addition to all this they have fun.

With the Soviet All Artists' Union, the IAAA is participating in 'Dialogues: Communication Through the Art of the Cosmos', a five-year project partly sponsored by the Planetary Society to enable artists of various countries to meet and work together. It culminates in a major Western/Soviet art exhibition (containing some of the work in this book), touring internationally from 1989 to 1992. The final painting, 'Together We Can . . .' by Beth Avary, encapsulates its spirit far better than more words.

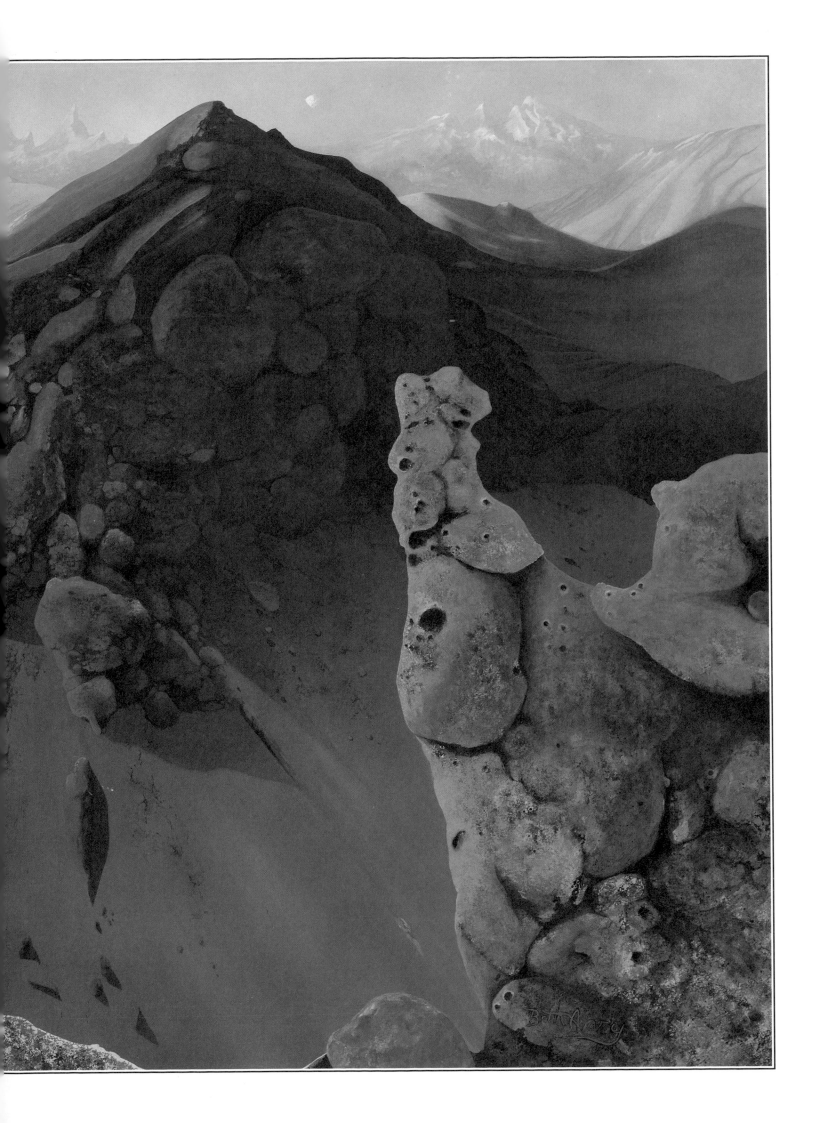

Index of Artists

(Italic figures indicate an Artist Profile)

Author's Acknowledgements

My grateful thanks go to the following for assistance in compiling this book — for providing addresses, obtaining transparencies, giving or obtaining permission for reproduction, and general help:

The IAAA and its members; Frederick C. Durant, III; Alexander A. Kulechow (Moscow) for the photographs of artwork by Leonov and Sokolov; Ron Miller; Kim P. Poor; Fred Clarke; Dr Chriet Titulaer; Mr Shigeru Komori; Dr Jean-Louis Heudier; Len Carter of the British Interplanetary Society; Louis Friedman of the Planetary Society; Frederick I. Ordway, III; Randy Lieberman; James E. Oberg; Uwe Luserke; Jack Moorby; Trish Burgess; National Geographic Society; Orbital Sciences Corporation; Boeing Aerospace; Eagle Engineering; to *New Scientist* for publishing the article (9 June 1988) that started it all rolling; and all individual artists concerned for their cooperation and encouragement.

Also to my trusty Atari ST; my wife, Ruth, for reading and checking the manuscript, compiling the index, making coffee to order and tolerating my glazed expression and late nights while I was working on this volume. And finally to Hubert Schaafsma and all at Dragon's World for their efficient help at every stage, and for making it possible for me to produce the book that I have always wanted on my own shelf.

My thanks do *not* go to certain organizations and postal services which failed to reply to requests and/or made it impossible for the work of certain excellent Soviet (and one or two US) artists to be included. Next edition, perhaps . . .?

Bibliography

Below is a list of the books mentioned in the text. While every endeavour has been made to obtain full details, some gaps, unfortunately, still exist. The publisher invites readers to submit any relevant information for inclusion in future reprints.

A Day in the Moon, Abbé Théophile Moreux (Hutchinson, 1913)

Across the Space Frontier, ed. *Collier's* magazine staff (Viking Press, New York, 1952; Sidgwick & Jackson, London, 1953)

The Answers to the Space Flight Challenge, Frank Tinsley (Whitestone Publications, 1958)

Ardneh's World ('Empire of the East' series, vol. III), Fred Saberhagen (Baen Books, 1988)

The Art of Science Fiction, Frank Kelly Freas (Donning Co., 1979)

Artistic Voyage Through Space and Nature, Kazuaki Iwasaki (Japan, 1987)

Astounding Fifties, Frank Kelly Freas (USA)

Astronomy: The Cosmic Journey, William K. Hartmann (Wadsworth, 1978)

Atlas of the Solar System, David A. Hardy (World's Work/Heinemann, 1982; revised edition, Octopus, 1986)

Beginnings, Gordon R. Dickson (Baen Books, 1988)

Beyond Gravity, Justin Leiber (Tor Books, 1988)

Beyond Spaceship Earth: Environmental Ethics and the Solar System, ed. Eugene C. Hargrove (Sierra Club, 1987)

Bildatlas des Sonnensystems (Atlas of the Solar System), Bruno Stanek and Ludek Pesek (Hallwag, 1974)

Broca's Brain: Reflections on the Romance of Science, Carl Sagan (Random House, 1979)

Challenge of the Stars, Patrick Moore and David A. Hardy (Mitchell Beazley, London, and Rand McNally, Chicago, 1972)

Chroma, Jon Gustafson (Father Tree Press, 1986)

Colonies in Space, T. A. Heppenheimer (Stackpole Books, 1978)

Conquest of the Moon (published as **Man on the Moon** in UK), Wernher von Braun, Fred L. Whipple and Willy Ley (Viking Press, New York, 1952; Sidgwick & Jackson, London, 1953)

The Conquest of Space, Willy Ley and Chesley Bonestell (Viking Press, New York, 1949; Sidgwick & Jackson, London, 1950)

Comet, Carl Sagan (Random House, New York, and Michael Joseph, London, 1985)

Contact, Carl Sagan (Simon & Schuster, New York, 1985; Century, London, 1986)

The Cosmic Connection, Carl Sagan (Doubleday, 1973)

Cosmos, Carl Sagan (Random House, New York, 1980; Futura, London, 1983)

Cycles of Fire, Ron Miller, William K. Hartmann and Pamela Lee (Workman, New York, 1987; Aurum, London, 1988)

The Dragons of Eden, Carl Sagan (Random House, 1977)

The Earth Is Near, Ludek Pesek (Bradbury Press, 1974)

L'Encyclopédie Larousse de l'astronomie (Larousse Encyclopedia of Astronomy), Lucien Rudaux and Gérard de Vaucouleurs (Larousse, 1948)

The Exploration of Mars, Willy Ley, Wernher von Braun and Chesley Bonestell (Viking, 1956)

The Exploration of Space, Arthur C. Clarke (Temple Press, 1951)

Exploration of the Moon, Arthur C. Clarke (Frederick Muller, 1954)

Exploring Our Solar System (Time-Life Books)

Exploring Your Solar System (National Geographic)

Fahrenheit 451, Ray Bradbury (Hart-Davis, 1954)

From Earth to the Moon, Jules Verne (J. B. Lippincott Co., 1865)

Galactic Tours, David A. Hardy and Bob Shaw (Proteus, 1981)

Galaxies, Lilika Papanicolaou (published privately, 1981)

The Grand Tour, Ron Miller and William K. Hartmann (Workman, 1981)

The Great Book of Planets, Chriet Titulaer (Strengholt)

The High Frontier, Gerard K. O'Neill (Morrow, 1977/Space Studies Institute, 1989)

High Road to the Moon, Bob Parkinson (British Interplanetary Society, 1979)

How to Study the Stars, Lucien Rudaux (T. Fisher Unwin, 1909)

Human Structure, M. Cartmill (Harvard University Press, 1987)

Industrialization of the Solar System (NASA, 1984)

Interplanetary Flight, Arthur C. Clarke (Temple Press, 1950)

Journey to the Planets, Peter Ryan (Penguin, 1972)

'Library of the Universe' series, Isaac Asimov (Gareth Stevens Inc., 1987–)

Log of a Moon Expedition, Ludek Pesek (Collins, 1967)

The Macmillan Book of Astronomy, Roy A. Gallant (Macmillan, 1986)

Man and the Planets, Duncan Lunan (Ashgrove Press, 1983)

Man and the Stars, Duncan Lunan (Souvenir Press, 1974)

Le Manuel pratique d'astronomie (Practical Manual of Astronomy), Lucien Rudaux (France, 1925)

Mars 1999: Exclusive Preview of the US/Soviet Manned Mission, Brian O'Leary (Stackpole Books, 1987)

Meteorites and Their Parent Planets, Harry Y. McSween (Cambridge University Press, 1987)

The Moon, James Nasmyth and James Carpenter (John Murray, 1874)

The Moon and Planets, Ludek Pesek and Josef Sadil (Hamlyn, 1963)

Moonwalk (Random House, 1989)

The New Astronomy, Nigel Henbest and Michael Marten (Cambridge University Press, 1983)

New Challenge of the Stars, Patrick Moore and David A. Hardy (Mitchell Beazley, London, and Rand McNally, Chicago, 1978)

New Destinies III and **IV**, ed. James Baen (Baen Books, 1988)

New Earths, James E. Oberg (New American Library, 1981)

The New Solar System, ed. Brian O'Leary and J. Kelly Beatty (Sky Publishing Corporation, 1981)

New Worlds for Old, Duncan Lunan (David & Charles, 1979)

Nine Planets, Alan E. Nourse (Harper & Row, 1960)

The Ocean World, Peter Ryan (Penguin, 1973)

Omni Space Almanac, Neil McAleer (Pharos Books, 1987)

Our Planet Earth, Ludek Pesek and Josef Sadil (Hamlyn, 1967)

Our Universe, Roy A. Gallant (National Geographic Society, 1980)

Our World in Space, Robert McCall and Isaac Asimov (Patrick Stephens, 1974)

Out of the Cradle, Ron Miller, William K. Hartmann and Pamela Lee (Workman, 1984)

Pioneering the Space Frontier, The Report of the National Commission on Space (Bantam, 1986)

Planet Earth, Peter Ryan (Penguin, 1972)

The Planets, ed. Byron Preiss (Bantam, 1985)

The Race to Mars, Frank Miles and Nicholas Booth (ITN/Macmillan, London, and Harper & Row, New York, 1988)

Raintree Illustrated Encyclopedia of Science (Raintree, 1984)

Rockets, Jets, Guided Missiles and Space Ships, Fletcher Pratt and Jack Coggins (Random House, New York, and Sidgwick & Jackson, London, 1951)

Science and Future Annual (Encyclopaedia Brittanica, 1970–)
The Search for Extraterrestrial Intelligence, Thomas R. McDonough (Wiley, 1986)
A Separate Star, Frank Kelly Freas (Greenswamp, 1985)
Society of Illustrators' 28th Annual, ed. Arpi Ermoyan (Madison Square, 1988)
Solar System, Peter Ryan and Ludek Pesek (Allen Lane, 1978)
Solar System, 'Planet Earth' series (Time-Life, 1983–)
Space: The Next 25 Years, Thomas R. McDonough (Wiley, 1987)
Space Art, Ron Miller (Workman, 1978)
The Space Encyclopedia (University of Rome Press, 1987)
Space Shuttles, Ludek Pesek and Bruno Stanek (Switzerland, 1976)
Spaceworks Calendar (Thomasson-Grant Inc., 1989)
Splendour of the Heavens (Hutchinson, 1923)
Suns, Myths and Men, Patrick Moore (Frederick Muller, 1954)
Sur les autres mondes (On Other Worlds), Lucien Rudaux (Larousse, 1937)
This Is Cosmos, Kazuaki Iwasaki (Japan, 1956)
Toward Distant Suns, T. A. Heppenheimer (Stackpole Books, 1979)
Twice in Time, Manly W. Wellman (Baen Books, 1988)
2001: A Space Odyssey, Arthur C. Clarke (Hutchinson, 1968)
UFOs and Other Worlds, Peter Ryan (Penguin, 1975)
Universe, Don Dixon (Houghton Mifflin, 1981)
The Universe, ed. Byron Preiss (Bantam, 1987)
The Universe and Beyond, Dickenson (USA)
Visions of the Future, Robert McCall and Ben Bova (Abrams, 1982)
Visions of the Universe, Isaac Asimov and Kazuaki Iwasaki (Cosmos Store, 1981)
Welcome to Mars, Ben Bova (USA)
World Book Encyclopedia (World Books, 1986)
World Book Encyclopedia Year Book (World Books, 1986)
The World We Live In (Time-Life, 1952)
Worlds Beyond: The Art of Chesley Bonestell, Frederick C. Durant, III and Ron Miller (Donning, 1983)
You Will Go to the Moon, Mae and Ira Freeman (Collins, 1959)

International Organizations and Societies

British Interplanetary Society
27/29 South Lambeth Road, London SW8 1SZ, England
Publishers of High Road to the Moon *and* Spaceflight *magazine; curators of R. A. Smith artwork, etc.*

International Association for the Astronomical Arts
PO Box 1584, New York City, NY 10011, USA
Non-profit organization devoted to promoting space art, exhibitions, international workshops, etc. Associate and Active grades available.

National Space Society
922 Pennsylvania Avenue SE, Washington, DC, USA
Publishers of Ad Astra; *promoters of space exploration; information source.*

The Planetary Society
65 North Carolina Avenue, Pasadena, California 91106, USA
Publishers of The Planetary Report; *campaigners for international space exploration, organizers of exhibitions, scholarships, conferences, contests, etc.*

Selected Sources for Prints, Postcards, Slides, etc. of Space Art

Astro Art
99 Southam Road, Hall Green, Birmingham B28 OAB, England
Slide sets, books and colour photo-prints from artwork by David A. Hardy. Lectures arranged; also transparency library. (Correspondence for any artist included in this book will be forwarded by Astro Art, providing postage is included. For US artists, it may be advisable to contact the IAAA first.)

Novagraphics
PO Box 37197, Tucson, Arizona 85740, USA
Fine art prints by Kim P. Poor and many other artists; also originals, posters, cards, etc. Colour catalogue available for customers.

Space Art International
109 Grafton Street, Chevy Chase Village, Maryland 20815, USA
Curators for the paintings of Bonestell, Iwasaki, Papanicolaou, Leonov, Miller, Pesek, Sokolov, and other artists. Transparency library.

Science Graphics
PO Box 7516, Bend, Oregon 97708, USA
Teaching slides, including sets of astronomical art by well-known artists.